Praise for *The*

"Read this book carefull[...] at what it means to be an emotionally and spiritually healthy human being who can love nonviolently."

> **Sally K. Severino, MD,** professor emeritus of psychiatry, University of New Mexico Health Sciences Center, and author of *Behold Our Moral Body: Psychiatry, Duns Scotus, and Neuroscience* and *Becoming Fire: A Freudian Psychoanalyst's Spiritual Journey*

"In *The Gospel According to St. Thérèse*, Br. Joseph Schmidt helps us encounter the extraordinary 'science of love' that was the lived faith of the beloved St. Thérèse. And he has crafted it precisely as Thérèse would have appreciated—as a resource for people to share their faith together, inspired by her 'little way' of spirituality. Her focus on the historical Jesus as the source and model of her own faith surely anticipated the pontificate of Pope Francis. This is truly a rich and timely resource."

> **Thomas Groome,** professor of theology and religious education, director of Boston College's Church in the 21st Century Center, and author of *What Makes Us Catholic: Eight Gifts for Life* and *Will There Be Faith? A New Vision for Educating and Growing Disciples*

"Illumined by the word of God, St. Thérèse's sometimes rugged path toward inner freedom and peace is invitingly described by Br. Joseph Schmidt. Those who accept this challenge will contribute greatly to world peace!"

> **Sr. Mary Grace, O Carm,** Vicar Prioress, Carmel of Our Lady of Grace, Christoval, Texas

"This is a beautiful book that will inspire readers to embrace the spirituality of the Little Flower. Br. Joseph Schmidt offers great insight into Thérèse's call for nonviolence to oneself and to others—a timely challenge in today's world. The book should be read slowly in order to savor the richness of trusting in God's mercy, forgiveness, and unconditional love. The *Gospel According to St. Thérèse* helps us understand why Pope St. John Paul described St. Thérèse's as 'the living icon of God.'"

Br. Bernard LoCoco, FSC, past president of Christian Brothers University, Memphis; former director of SAT Sabbatical Program in Berkeley, California; and currently a spiritual director and teacher in spirituality

"St. Thérèse of Lisieux is the apostle of interpersonal, nonviolent love—what she called 'the science of love'—and Br. Joseph Schmidt is one of the best teachers of Thérèse's little way of nonviolent love writing in English today. *The Gospel According to St. Thérèse* should be read prayerfully and reread often so that we, too, might renounce the little jabs of violence, retaliation, and retribution and become saints and scientists of nonviolent love."

Fr. John Dear, a coordinator with Pace e Bene, and author of thirty-five books on peace and nonviolence, including *The Questions of Jesus* and *The Beatitudes of Peace*

"By naming Thérèse a doctor of the Church, Pope St. John Paul II 'attested to the authenticity of her Gospel for our time.' Br. Joseph Schmidt's genius has been to explore and articulate Thérèse's spirituality of creative nonviolent love. *The Gospel According to St. Thérèse: A Faith-Sharing Guide* continues this vitally important work. Br. Joseph is always meaty, always intriguing. How much those of us who love Thérèse owe to him."

    Heather King, author of *Shirt of Flame: A Year with St. Thérèse of Lisieux*

"Br. Joseph Schmidt's profound insights into the life and spirituality of St. Thérèse permeate his new book. It is like a meditation that plumbs the depth of her Gospel 'little way' spirituality. When Pope St. John Paul II declared Thérèse a Doctor of the Church, he basically told us to read the Gospels through her eyes and heart. *The Gospel According to St. Thérèse* helps us understand our inner experience of God's love and mercy. It is a real gem!"

    Fr. Bob Colaresi, O Carm, Society of the Little Flower, Darien, Illinois

THE GOSPEL ACCORDING TO ST. THÉRÈSE

A Faith-Sharing Guide

Joseph F. Schmidt, FSC

Copyright @ 2017 Brothers of the Christian Schools

Published by The Word Among Us Press
7115 Guilford Drive, Suite 100
Frederick, Maryland 21704
www.wau.org

21 20 19 18 17   1 2 3 4 5

ISBN: 978-1-59325-315-8
eISBN: 978-1-59325-497-1

Additional acknowledgments begin on page 158.

Cover design by Coronation Media
Cover art copyright © Office Central de Lisieux

Made and printed in the United States of America

Library of Congress Control Number: 2017949369

Contents

Other Books by Joseph F. Schmidt, FSC

Praying Our Experiences:
An Invitation to Open Our Lives to God

Praying with Thérèse of Lisieux

Everything Is Grace:
The Life and Way of Thérèse of Lisieux

Walking the Little Way of Thérèse of Lisieux:
Discovering the Path of Love

A Note about Thérèse's Words

The words Thérèse underlined in her writing are in italics; the words she capitalized are in uppercase.

A Note about the Scripture Translations

All Scripture translations are from the New Revised Standard Version, Catholic Edition (NRSVCE) unless indicated as Douay-Rheims (DR). The Douay-Rheims is an English version of the French translation that is close to the translation Thérèse herself might have used.

Source Abbreviations

CCC: *Catechism of the Catholic Church*

DAS: *Divini Amoris Scientia,* Apostolic Letter of His Holiness Pope John Paul II Proclaiming St. Thérèse a Doctor of the Church

EIG: *Everything Is Grace: The Life and Way of Thérèse of Lisieux* by Joseph F. Schmidt, FSC

FGM: *Saint Thérèse of Lisieux: Her Family, Her God, Her Message* by Bernard Bro, OP

GC: *General Correspondence, Volumes 1 and 2,* translated by John Clarke, OCD

HLC: *St. Thérèse of Lisieux: Her Last Conversations,* translated by John Clarke, OCD

SS: *Story of a Soul: The Autobiography of St. Thérèse of Lisieux,* third edition, translated by John Clarke, OCD

STL: *St. Thérèse of Lisieux by Those Who Knew Her,* edited and translated by Christopher O'Mahony, OCD

TLMT: *Thérèse of Lisieux and Marie of the Trinity* by Pierre Descouvemont

WLW: *Walking the Little Way of Thérèse of Lisieux: Discovering the Path of Love* by Joseph F. Schmidt, FSC

Introduction

It is possible to write a convincing book about China without ever having visited the vast and beautiful country. It is possible to speak compellingly about the realities of the Gospel text without ever having had an experience of Jesus' authentic good news. With Thérèse things are different. She speaks from the few outer geographical places and the many inner spiritual spaces that she has personally visited. From her own lived experience, and not from theological treatises or faith hearsay, she proclaimed the true God and the authentic Gospel (see FGM 10–11).

Thus Pope St. John Paul II could rightly say, "One can say with conviction about Thérèse of Lisieux that the Spirit of God allowed her heart to reveal directly to the people of our time the *fundamental mystery,* the reality of the Gospel. . . . Her 'little way' is the way of 'holy childhood'" (DAS 10).

The Gospel According to St. Thérèse attempts to express the essence of the Gospel revelation of Jesus as Thérèse of Lisieux—also popularly known as Thérèse of the Child Jesus or the Little Flower—lived and taught that good news. The book offers a very brief introduction to the fundamental faith vision and wisdom of Thérèse by

- identifying some of Thérèse's writings that conveyed important aspects of her spiritual insights;

- noting the process by which Thérèse used Scripture as the light and mirror to see more clearly, critique, and deepen the intuitive understanding of her own experiences;
- pointing out passages of Scripture that Thérèse wove into some of her writings, and
- providing questions for personal reflection and small-group faith sharing to help readers implement Thérèse's teaching in their own lives.

With this focus and method, *The Gospel According to St. Thérèse* supplements and summarizes two previous books that are more extensive in scope and more narrative in style: *Everything Is Grace* (2007) and *Walking the Little Way of Thérèse of Lisieux* (2012).

There is, of course, no better way to understand the depth of Thérèse's wisdom, appreciate her human and spiritual struggles, and notice the developmental nature of her faith vision than to read her own writings. Particularly important are her memoir, *Story of a Soul*, and her letters.

Each session of *The Gospel According to St. Thérèse* centers on a particular theme of Thérèse's spiritual teaching and focuses on the awareness she gained through the interaction of what she learned from her own experiences and what she understood from the Scriptures. Thérèse continually contemplated her experiences, wondering and questioning their meaning. She also meditated on the Scriptures and established a dialogue between her own experiences and the Scriptures that touched her.

When, at the very young age of twenty—having entered the community at Lisieux only five years before, in 1888, at age fifteen—she was assigned to teach spirituality to new members of the Carmelite community, she encouraged the sisters to contemplate their own lives and the Scripture in a similar dialogic way. Her teaching methods were often question-discussion sessions or group interactive approaches. She did not impose her spirituality or try to make others into her own image. Noting that *"there are really more differences among souls than there are among faces,"* Thérèse respected God's unique call to each (see SS 239). Her teaching is without imposition; it is all invitation.

* * * * * *

There is only one Gospel, of course, and so we speak of *the* Gospel and not the *Gospels* according to Matthew, Mark, Luke, and John. The *one* Gospel is the good news, revealing God's inclusive, enduring, nonviolent love, which Jesus personifies. But it is also appropriate to speak of the Gospel *according* to Thérèse, because in her unique and limited way, she expressed Jesus' revelation, as did each of the Evangelists, with the guidance of the Holy Spirit, within the developing tradition of the Church, and in conformity with the times.

In 1997, the hundredth anniversary of Thérèse's death, Pope St. John Paul II proclaimed her a doctor of the Church. In *Divini Amoris Scientia* (DAS), the document naming her a doctor, he stated, "She has made the Gospel shine appealingly in our time." "One can say with conviction about Thérèse of Lisieux," the pope added, "that the Spirit of God allowed her heart to reveal directly to the people of our time the fundamental mystery, the reality of the Gospel" (DAS 8, 10). By naming Thérèse a doctor, the pope attested to the authenticity of *her* Gospel for *our* time.

Pope St. John Paul added that Thérèse's spirituality is especially *"timely"* (DAS 11) because she brings forward into our day the message of God's love by living that message with the mentality and with the concerns, usual feelings, gifts, and weaknesses of ordinary people today. As well as she could, but quite imperfectly, she lived Gospel love, particularly as she dealt with difficult people and painful circumstances.

In this present era of such personal and cultural violence, Thérèse makes Gospel love understandable and acceptable to people by modeling the meaning, beauty, and truth of being loved by God and empowered to love as God loves. She lets us glimpse a person who lived life well, a human saint who lived God's nonviolent love yet was never completely free from personal emotional and spiritual limitations common in the lives of many in these days. In this she gives us healing and hope.

Pope St. John Paul II noted that Thérèse's life and teaching are particularly consoling and hopeful as well as challenging today for several reasons:

- "Thérèse is a *woman*, who in approaching the Gospel knew how to grasp its hidden wealth with that practicality and deep resonance of life and wisdom which belong to the feminine genius" (DAS 11). Thus her life and teaching complement the more extensive work of male theologians that has filled theology and spirituality from the beginning of the Church.
- "Thérèse is also a *contemplative*," the pope wrote. "By her life Thérèse offers a witness and theological illustration of the beauty of the contemplative life as the total dedication to Christ" (DAS 11). That is, she manifests, in ordinary life experiences, the contemplative spirit—the spirit of faith—a faith vision that allowed her to see with God's vision of love and to do what she thought was God's will. In the simplicity

and imperfections of her life, and in her willingness to love God, herself, and others with patience and kindness, with perseverance and truth, without retaliation or violence, she modeled the power of love and invites everyone to affirm "God's primacy over all things" (DAS 11).

- "Thérèse of Lisieux is a *young person*," the pope noted, bringing to her encounter with the Gospel "a fresh and original vision, presenting a teaching of eminent quality" (DAS 11, 8). The passion of youth, so often squandered in grasping substitute fulfillment, Thérèse fulfilled in passion's true destiny—union with God in Christ Jesus—thereby discovering the meaning of her life. She found the pearl of great price, the treasure hidden in the field, and she sold all (see Matthew 13:44-46).

Thérèse is also a timely spiritual instructor because, by her teaching and life, she addressed a major issue of contemporary theology and spirituality. She contributed uniquely to the developing consciousness that holiness is not to be mystified by false asceticism, moralistic perfectionism, religious rituals, and doctrinal notions. Such mystification lifted sanctity three inches off the ground, rejecting common humanity and making goodness and holiness mostly unintelligible and inaccessible to ordinary people. By living precisely on the ground of her humanity, with her emotional and personal gifts and imperfections, Thérèse brought an authenticity, an integrity, and a unity to living little and living great, to living passionately and living well, to living in joy and living in holiness, and to living Gospel love and living fully human.

In short, the dynamics of Thérèse's life, which she shared so truthfully, simply, and transparently in her writings, reveal what it might look like to be a good and holy person today. Her writings expose the interior state, the thoughts and feelings, the successes and failures, the inner and outer practices, of a modern person living life well. This is a great gift to the Church, which, while reiterating traditional rituals, dogmas, and morals, still struggles to articulate the answer to common contemporary spiritual questions: "How does a contemporary saint think, feel, and act?" "What does Gospel goodness and authentic Christian holiness look like in modern times?"

Thérèse's life is a great gift to each member of the mystical body of Christ perplexed by these same spiritual questions and yet desiring to be filled more deeply with God's own love, life, peace, and joy. Thus Pope St. John Paul II concludes that Thérèse "appears as a Teacher of evangelical life" (DAS 11)—the life of goodness, founded on the good news proclaimed to everyone, the invitation to welcome God's love and to live God's love without violence or retaliation, which Jesus personifies in the Gospels.

Session 1

THE GOSPEL ACCORDING TO ST. THÉRÈSE

Sacred Scripture

I came that they may have life, and have it abundantly. (John 10:10)

See that none of you repays evil for evil, but always seek to do good to one another and to all. (1 Thessalonians 5:15)

"For who has known the mind of the Lord
   so as to instruct him?"
But we have the mind of Christ. (1 Corinthians 2:16)

He is kind to the ungrateful and the wicked. Be merciful, just as your Father is merciful. (Luke 6:35-36)

Many waters cannot quench love,
   neither can floods drown it.
If one offered for love
   all the wealth of one's house,
   it would be utterly scorned. (Song of Solomon 8:7)

For "In him [God] we live and move and have our being." (Acts 17:28)

The kingdom of God is within you. (Luke 17:21, DR)

Words of St. Thérèse

Ah! how many lights have I not drawn from the Works of our holy Father, St. John of the Cross! At the ages of seventeen and eighteen I had no other spiritual nourishment; later on, however, all books left me in aridity and I'm still in that state. If I open a book composed by a spiritual author (even the most beautiful, the most touching book), I feel my heart contract immediately and I read without understanding, so to speak. Or if I do understand, my mind comes to a standstill without the capacity of meditating. In this helplessness . . . it is especially the *Gospels* which sustain me during my hours of prayer, for in them I find what is necessary for my poor little soul. I am constantly discovering in them new lights, hidden and mysterious meanings.

I understand and I know from experience that: *"The kingdom of God is within you."* Jesus has no need of books or teachers to instruct souls; He teaches without the noise of words. Never have I heard Him speak, but I feel that He is within me at each moment; He is guiding and inspiring me with what I must say and do. I find just when I need them certain lights [insights] which I had not seen until then, and it isn't most frequently during my hours of prayer that these are most abundant but rather in the midst of my daily occupations.

—*Story of a Soul,* 179

Consider!

Thérèse joined an elite group of then only thirty-two other theologians and spiritual teachers, in the entire history of the Church, when Pope St. John Paul II proclaimed her a doctor of the Church. She is the most contemporary of the doctors—if she had lived to be ninety, an age two of her blood sisters reached, she would have died in 1963. Thérèse is also the youngest doctor, having died at the age of twenty-four.

The honor of doctor has made Thérèse the peer of such eminent spiritual and theological giants as John Chrysostom, Jerome, Augustine, Thomas Aquinas, Bonaventure, Francis de Sales, Teresa of Avila, John of the Cross, and Alphonsus Liguori. Why would so great an honor be given to such a "little soul," "a little flower," as Thérèse called herself? The pope answered that question in *Divini Amoris Scientia*. Among the reasons he gave were these:

- "Thérèse is a Teacher for our time, which thirsts for living and essential words, for heroic and credible acts of witness" (DAS 11).
- Thérèse is "loved and accepted by brothers and sisters of other Christian communities and even by non-Christians" (DAS 11).
- "A *particular radiance of doctrine* shines forth from her writings which, as if by a charism of the Holy Spirit, grasp the very heart of the message of Revelation" (DAS 8).

- "With her distinctive doctrine and unmistakable style, Thérèse appears as an *authentic teacher of faith and the Christian life*" (DAS 8).

These were astonishing statements for Pope St. John Paul II to make about a saint without academic credentials and with no exceptional works.

This session and the following sessions attempt to cast light on the meaning of these and other praises from all the popes since her death, as well as adulations from spiritual leaders of many denominations and vast numbers of other "little souls."

* * * * * *

Thérèse never had access to the entire Bible. The spirituality of her time discouraged the ordinary faithful from reading the Bible, especially the Old Testament, fearing the text would be misinterpreted. Céline, Thérèse's older sister, who entered Carmel after Thérèse, copied some Old Testament texts from their uncle's Bible and shared these with Thérèse. Especially in some of the writings of Isaiah, Proverbs, the psalms, and the Canticle of Canticles, Thérèse discovered confirmation of her spiritual intuitions, and these texts were important in establishing her faith vision.

Despite her limited reading of the Bible and her lack of any formal scriptural studies—Thérèse never even "graduated" from grade school—she referred in her writings to more than four hundred texts of the Old Testament and over six hundred from the New Testament. She quoted mostly from memory and not always with perfect accuracy. She was bold and original, creatively interpreting, interrelating, and recognizing practical applications in the scriptural texts. She confidently relied on the wisdom she continually gained from the contemplation of her own experience in light of the texts that spoke to her.

* * * * * *

Thérèse discovered her "little way," as she called her spirituality, only gradually over her lifetime, with scant help from the spirituality of her day. The preaching she heard and the spiritual direction she received were of little assistance to her because they carried mistaken ideas that contradicted Gospel revelation.

Focusing her contemplation on the Gospel, particularly on Jesus, and also on the writings and work of St. Paul, Thérèse recognized the characteristics of Jesus' love and the love of Jesus' Father. She tried to cultivate these characteristics in her own heart: inner freedom, by resisting the oppression of excessive feelings and compulsive thoughts; compassion, by respecting others on their terms; creativity, by being adaptable to others and to circumstances she could not improve; willingness, by not bullying herself or others. She practiced self-surrender in the reality of the present moment and gratitude for the inner gift of each experience.

Thérèse understood that if these qualities were in her heart, her love became Jesus-like, godlike: patient, kind, inclusive, and without retaliation or violence. These psychological-spiritual qualities helped her heart participate in the mind and heart of Christ.

Understanding and practicing these human heart qualities became what Thérèse called "the science of Love." Discovering this science was her lifelong quest. Toward the end of her life, she wrote, "Ah, yes, this word [love] resounds sweetly in the ear of my soul, and I desire only this science" (SS 187, 188).

Contemplating Jesus, the love of God incarnate, Thérèse saw that Jesus did not hold grudges or retaliate. He was not punitive or vindictive, but as he said, "I came that they may have life, and have it abundantly" (John 10:10). Imitating Jesus by cultivating the flourishing of life through the practice of the heart qualities of love—loving without violence to herself or her sisters, and even in the broken situations in which she found herself—became the central teaching of Thérèse's spirituality.

Intuitively Thérèse knew that Jesus' message of nonviolent love was not being taught in the spirituality of her time. The understanding of holiness in her birthplace, France, as well as in much of Western Europe—even in Thérèse's Carmelite community—was contaminated by the heresies of Jansenism and Pelagianism and poisoned by a spirit of moral perfectionism.

Thérèse recognized that it was not true to portray God as vindictive and violent—a mistake of Jansenism. She knew Jesus emphasized the practice of love and did not focus primarily on obedience to laws. Jesus welcomed sinners into a deeper love relationship with God, his Father. Thérèse also knew it was mistaken to think that holiness needed to be or could be achieved with human, willful effort alone—the errors of perfectionism and Pelagianism.

Throughout her life, Thérèse grew in the spirit of confidence and love, repenting in failure but not discouraged by imperfections and sins. In her maturity, she became convinced that a loving person may not always be morally perfect but could practice the self-discipline of dying daily to selfish interests and could act more and more charitably. She knew her passionate desire to become a loving person would never be fulfilled by the self-centered, willful striving to reach impossible moral perfection but only by drawing closer to the Source of Love through prayer and practice.

Thérèse's little way concentrated on doing everything in a spirit of faith and charity, inconspicuously and as each moment required. Jesus, she noticed, lived and acted lovingly at every moment, calling and empowering his followers to do likewise.

When proclaiming Thérèse a doctor of the Church, Pope St. John Paul II affirmed that she had grasped the science of love: "During her life Thérèse discovered . . . that 'science of love' which she then expressed with particular originality in her writings" (DAS 1).

As she walked her path of love, Thérèse's life and teaching converged into a unique manifestation of what a loving person, a godlike person, looks like today. Thérèse, Pope St. John Paul II said, is "a living icon of that God who . . . 'shows his almighty power in his mercy and forgiveness'" (DAS 8, quoting the Roman Missal). Thérèse is a "Teacher for our time," the pope continued, modeling "the most genuine spiritual life, presented to all the faithful in a living, accessible language" (DAS 11, 8).

The great gift of Thérèse's life is her being a "living icon of God" and providing both a narrative and a portrait of how a contemporary saint—a loving, Christlike, godlike person—lives in the very common trials and joys of a very ordinary life. In this way, she affirms the traditional Church teaching that everyone, even a "little soul," is called to be a saint—not a canonized saint but a loving person, willingly enduring the inevitable pain of loving and gratefully appreciating the holy joy of sharing God's mercy and forgiveness.

Understand!

1. Thérèse said she knew from experience that "the kingdom of God" is within you (Luke 17:21). When Jesus made that point about the kingdom of God to his disciples, what do you think he meant? What do you think Thérèse meant?

   _____

   _____

   _____

   _____

   _____

2. When a particular Scripture verse caught Thérèse's eye, she considered the passage in light of her own experiences, letting a dialogue take place between the two. How does this approach—a dialogue between Scripture and personal experience—confirm or challenge your own way of understanding the passages of Scripture that strike you?

   _____

   _____

   _____

   _____

   _____

3. Jesus said that he came so that we might have life "abundantly" (John 10:10). Thérèse's understanding of abundant life included a rejection of the concept of violence to self and to

others. How do you think her dialogue with Scripture helped her to move beyond the harsh spirituality of her time?

_____

_____

_____

_____

_____

4. Consider Thérèse's statement that it was "*especially the Gospels*" that sustained her. How do the Gospels sustain you?

_____

_____

_____

_____

_____

Reflect!

1. Thérèse said that she tended to receive spiritual insights during her round of daily activities rather than during her prayer times. How might her experience help you be more open to God and more open to when and how you receive spiritual insights?

_____

_____

_____

_____

_____

2. A striking feature of Thérèse's life was her refusal to be discouraged by her imperfections. How do you handle discouragement? Which teachings of Thérèse might help you to live with greater hope when you are discouraged by your imperfections or the imperfections of others?

_____

_____

_____

_____

_____

3. Pope St. John Paul II identified Thérèse as "a living icon" of God. What heart qualities do you think she discovered in Jesus and made her own, transforming her into that icon? Do all of us have the potential to become icons of God?

_____

_____

_____

_____

_____

4. What blessings have you received through Thérèse's intercession, fulfilling her famous promise to spend her heaven doing good on earth? Do you know of blessings that others have received?

_____

_____

_____

_____

_____

Act!

In what ways does the assurance that God's love is without violence and that Jesus asks us to love without violence, challenge you personally?

Session 2

THE STORY OF GOD'S MERCY

Sacred Scripture

It is good . . . to acknowledge and reveal the works of God, and with fitting honor to acknowledge him. (Tobit 12:7)

Say to the just man that it is well. (Isaiah 3:10, DR)

The mercies of the Lord I will sing for ever. (Psalm 88:2, DR)

[Jesus] went up the mountain and called to him those whom he wanted. (Mark 3:13)

For he says to Moses,
   "I will have mercy on whom I have mercy,
   and I will have compassion on whom I have compassion."
So it depends not on human will or exertion, but on God who shows mercy. (Romans 9:15-16)

   The Lord is my shepherd, I shall not want. . . .
      he restores my soul.
   He leads me in right paths
      for his name's sake.
   Even though I walk through the darkest valley,
      I fear no evil;
   for you are with me. (Psalm 23:1, 3-4)

The LORD is merciful and gracious,
    slow to anger and abounding in steadfast love.
(Psalm 103:8)

If you then, who are evil, know how to give good gifts to your children, how much more will your Father in heaven give good things to those who ask him! (Matthew 7:11)

Go and learn what this means, "I desire mercy, not sacrifice." For I have come to call not the righteous but sinners. (Matthew 9:13)

Words of St. Thérèse

It is to you, dear Mother, to you who are doubly my Mother, that I come to confide the story of my soul. The day you asked me to do this [writing], it seemed to me it would distract my heart by too much concentration on myself, but since then Jesus has made me feel that in obeying simply, I would be pleasing Him; besides, I'm going to be doing only one thing: I shall begin to sing what I must sing eternally: *"The Mercies of the Lord."* . . .

I was surprised when I saw Him shower His extraordinary favors on saints who had offended Him, for instance, St. Paul and St. Augustine. . . . I wondered why [some poor people] died . . . without even having heard the name of God pronounced.

Jesus deigned to teach me this mystery. He set before me the book of nature; I understood how all the flowers He has created are beautiful, how the splendor of the rose . . . do[es] not take away . . . the delightful simplicity of the daisy. . . .

And so it is in the world of souls, Jesus' garden. He willed to create great souls . . . , but He has created smaller ones and these must be content to be daisies or violets destined to give joy to God's glances when He looks down at His feet. Perfection consists in doing His will, in being what He wills us to be.

I understood, too, that Our Lord's love is revealed as perfectly in the most simple soul that resists His grace in nothing as in the most excellent soul; in fact, since the nature of love is to humble oneself, if all souls resembled those of the holy Doctors who illumined the Church with the clarity of their teachings, it seems God would not descend so low when coming to their heart. But He created the child who knows only how to make his feeble cries heard; He has created the poor savage who has nothing but the natural law to guide him. It is to their hearts that God deigns to lower Himself. These are the wild flowers whose simplicity attracts Him. When coming down in this way, God manifests His infinite grandeur. Just as the sun shines simultaneously on the tall cedars and on each little flower as though it were alone on the earth, so Our Lord is occupied particularly with each soul as though there were no others like it . . . .

It is not, then, my life properly so-called that I am going to write; it is my *thoughts* on the graces God deigned to grant me. I find myself at a period in my life when I can cast a glance upon the past; my soul has matured in the crucible of exterior and interior trials. And now, like a flower strengthened by the storm, I can raise my head and see the words of Psalm 22 realized in me: "The Lord is my Shepherd, I shall not want." . . .

To me the Lord has always been "merciful and good, slow to anger and abounding in steadfast love."

It is with great happiness, then, that I come to sing the mercies of the Lord. . . .

The flower about to tell her story rejoices at . . . [proclaiming] the totally gratuitous gifts of Jesus. She knows . . . His mercy alone brought about everything that is good in her.

—*Story of a Soul,* 13–15

I know that without Him, I could have fallen as low as St. Mary Magdalene, . . . but I also know that Jesus has *forgiven me more* than *St. Mary Magdalene* since He forgave me *in advance* by preventing me from falling. Ah! I wish I could explain what I feel. Here is an example which will express my thoughts at least a little.

Suppose a clever physician's child meets with a stone in his path which causes him to fall and break a limb. His father comes to him immediately, picks him up lovingly, takes care of his hurt, using all the resources of his profession for this. His child, completely cured, shows his gratitude. This child is no doubt right in loving his father! But I am going to make another comparison. The father, knowing there is a stone in his child's way, hastens ahead of him and removes it but without anyone's seeing him do it. Certainly, this child, the object of his father's tender foresight, but *UNAWARE* of the misfortune from which he was delivered by him, will not thank him and *will love him less* than if he had been cured by him. But if he should come to learn the danger from which he escaped, *will he not love his father more*? Well, I am this child, the object of the *foreseeing love of a Father* who has not sent His Word to save the *just*, but *sinners*. He wants me *to love* Him because He *has forgiven* me not much but ALL. He has not expected me to *love Him much* like Mary Magdalene, but He has willed that I KNOW how He has loved me with a love of *unspeakable foresight* in order that now I may love Him unto *folly*!

—*Story of a Soul*, 83–84

Consider!

"It is to you, dear Mother, to you who are doubly my Mother, that I come to confide the story of my soul" (SS 13). With these words, Thérèse began writing her memoirs in early January 1895, just as she turned twenty-two years old. She had been in the Carmelite community for seven years and had about two and a half more years to live.

At a community recreation during the days of the 1894 Christmas festivities, Thérèse had been reminiscing with Pauline and Marie, her blood sisters with her in Carmel, about her life. Seeing Thérèse at her playful best as storyteller, humorist, and mimic, Marie commented to Pauline, the prioress at the time, that it would be especially regrettable to lose any of Thérèse's stories.

Marie knew of Thérèse's reluctance to promote herself, so she asked Pauline, who as "Mother" of the community was "doubly" Thérèse's mother, to ask their little sister to write about her childhood (HLC 231). At first Thérèse thought her sisters were joking, but Pauline gave Thérèse a more formal order.

Simply because of obedience, Thérèse began her writing, having only about an hour each evening. She did not use an outline and wrote spontaneously with few erasures. It is "as though I were fishing with a line: I write whatever comes to the end of my pen," she later said (HLC 63).

She finished this first and longest portion of her story (about 175 pages) by the end of the year. Subsequently two other shorter writings of Thérèse were added to this original manuscript, forming the current edition of her autobiography, *Story of a Soul.*

As Thérèse was living her life day by day, she experienced the ordinary trials and joys, the confusion and clarity, the disappointments, the fears and peace, that everyone seeking God experiences. But as she prayerfully reminisced, she recognized more clearly God's love permeating all her experiences; it was therefore from the point of view of God's merciful, forgiving love that Thérèse wrote.

Thérèse had experienced nothing extraordinary that might be expected of a canonized saint. Like the stories of innumerable men and women searching for authenticity, peace, and love, Thérèse's story is everyone's search for transcendence, for meaning, for God.

Beginning to write, Thérèse noted that when Pauline first asked her, it seemed that her writing would concentrate her thoughts too much on herself. She was well aware of her tendency toward self-centeredness and vanity. Later she remarked that some saints with a similar fear did not want to leave any writings, but others, like St. Teresa of Avila, followed the advice found in the Book of Tobit: have "no fears of revealing the secrets of [God] in order that they may make Him more loved and known by souls" (SS 207).

As for whether it is more pleasing to God to write personal memories or not, Thérèse believed that most important was obedience and following the inspiration of the Holy Spirit, since Isaiah wrote: *"Tell the just man ALL is well."* "Yes, all is well," Thérèse concluded, "when one seeks only the will of Jesus" (SS 207). Such sentiments inspired Thérèse to more wholeheartedly begin her writing.

Thérèse opened her memoirs by noting that her writing would be about only one thing. She would not be writing about herself but about the graces God granted her. By recalling her life, she was beginning to express the same gratitude that she would express forever in heaven—singing eternally "the mercies of the Lord" (SS 15).

After praying to the Virgin Mary, Thérèse opened the Gospel at random and chanced to read, "And going up a mountain, he called to him men of his *own choosing*, and they came to him" (SS 13). These words revealed the "mystery" of her whole life—the complete gratuity of God's love and her vocation to share God's love in a special way with the entire Church. At the end of her life, she did discover this special, mysterious vocation hidden within her vocation to Carmel: "MY VOCATION IS LOVE. . . . [I]n the heart of the Church, my Mother, I shall be *Love*" (SS 194).

Equally important to Thérèse were the words of St. Paul that summarized her life: "God will have mercy on whom he will have mercy" (see Romans 9:15). God's love is not the result of a person's human willfulness or schemes but of God showing mercy. With Paul, Thérèse believed she received God's infinite mercies, not by willful striving to become morally perfect, but by her faith, trust, prayer, and willing desire.

She did not wonder *if* God showed mercy to sinners but *why* God favored sinners, sometimes bestowing on them special graces. She pondered also why so many people died never hearing the name of God and so received God's mercy without having the joy of showing gratitude to the giver. To answer her concerns, Thérèse pondered her own experiences and the Gospel, contemplating how deeply mysterious and universally available God's mercy actually is.

* * * * * *

Before she was even three years old, Thérèse accompanied her father when he went fishing; these outings nourished her love of nature. The splendor and majesty of trees and the power and brilliance of lightning were particularly captivating to the young child. She was especially enchanted by the loveliness of each flower, from the largest and most robust to the smallest and most delicate.

During these early formative years, Thérèse's eyes were opened to the beauty of all of nature. She delighted in recognizing that every creature in its own way gave glory to God by being the creature that God willed it to be. This seminal idea helped her to know that holiness consisted in being willing and grateful to become who God wanted her to be.

Thérèse's early awareness that everything in the outside world was to be treasured also helped her value everything in her inner world and to respect the inner worlds of others as well. The seed had been sown for her understanding that the spiritual life had no home for comparisons or rivalries. Rather, holiness consisted in willingly welcoming her unique relationship with God.

"Perfection consists in doing His will, in being what He wills us to be," she wrote (SS 14).

Later, recognizing her inability to attain the kind of perfection taught in her day, Thérèse added, "I must bear with myself such as I am with all my imperfections" (SS 207). She could not be a great cedar of Lebanon. She would be a "little flower," in the lowest place, giving praise and thanksgiving to God, cooperating with God, who would make her his saint in his time.

For Thérèse to accept and appreciate herself as she was, and not to willfully strive to be what she could not be, was not an attitude of passivity. Rather, she saw that doing what God willed required active awareness, accepting her weakness, and willingly loving as God loves.

Obedience to God required her, as a loving person, to bear without bitterness or resentment the disappointment of her lingering imperfections. Thérèse recognized that holiness was to welcome as God's providence all that she could not change even in herself, even with her best intentions. This truth completely countered the spirituality taught in her time and became a significant part of Thérèse's little way. Ultimately, she desired to do God's will and get close to the Source of Love, even if that meant not getting close to achieving her spiritual ambitions.

Thérèse grasped another important truth about love. She saw that "the nature of love is to humble oneself" (SS 14). Even God lowered himself by loving into existence the lowly as well as the great. Thérèse believed that God's mercy is universal, like the light of the shining sun falling on every flower as well as on each cedar, as if each were special. She was convinced that everything worked in a special way for the good of each person.

Thérèse based her conviction on the spirit of faith. It assured her that the Lord, her good shepherd, had led her from the beginning and would continue to lead her safely through every trial and joy.

She recognized patience and kindness as components of God's mercy and love, uniquely directed to each person. Now, in her writings, she was going to describe as honestly as she could her experience of God's patient kindness toward her. She would not hide the blessings God had given her under a false humility. Rather, she would rejoice by showing that it was God's mercy alone that had brought about everything that was good in her.

* * * * * *

At the time she was writing, Thérèse was reaching full understanding of her little way of love. The words of Jesus affirmed her experience in her own family: if we, who are so imperfect, can be charitable to one another, how much more will God be generous to us. Thérèse had rested in the arms of her parents, and she was confident she would find love in the arms of God, who constantly reached toward her.

As she wrote her memoirs, she appreciated more and more God's mercy—always stooping down and patiently raising her up from her misery, at times even preventing her from falling. Later, referring to God's love, she wrote the parable comparing two ways a physician could help his little son. In the first scenario, the physician helps bring his son back to health after the child has fallen on a stone. In the second, the physician goes on the path before the son arrives and removes the stone. If this son never knew his father's tender foresight, he might love his father less than if he had been cured by him.

Thérèse had begun to recognize that she had been protected from many falls by the faith and love she experienced in her family life and in her Carmelite community. She was the child loved in advance by God and loved continuously by God even though she had fallen. God had forgiven her everything, always from the first with "foreseeing love." God, Thérèse believed, wanted her to know how much he had loved her "with a love of *unspeakable foresight* in order that now I may love Him unto *folly*!" (SS 84).

To discover the "science of love," and to love God to folly, became the passion of Thérèse's life.

Understand!

1. Thérèse read in Scripture that Jesus "called to him men of his *own choosing*, and they came to him" (see Mark 3:13). She herself felt unworthy of Jesus' call, but she understood that his call was mysterious and not based on worthiness. What stories from Scripture reinforce this point?

_____

_____

_____

_____

_____

2. Thérèse referred to Scripture when she wrote that the Father "has not sent His Word to save the *just*, but *sinners*" (see Matthew 9:13). Did Jesus exclude any types of sins or sinners from his statement? In what ways do you think this passage challenges Christians today?

_____

_____

_____

_____

_____

3. Psalm 103:8 tells us that God is not only merciful but also "slow to anger." How does Jesus reveal both mercy and anger in his ministry? When he does show anger, what is at the root of his distress (see Matthew 21:12-13; Mark 3:5)?

_____

_____

_____

_____

_____

4. In the middle of chaos and suffering, Isaiah tells the people that all will be well for the righteous (see Isaiah 3:10). When Thérèse quoted this passage, she had already experienced the "crucible . . . of trials," with worse to come. In what specific ways do you think the Bible encourages believers to thrive in the midst of suffering and hardship?

_____

_____

_____

_____

_____

Reflect!

1. With its emphasis on God's mercy, Thérèse's spirituality anticipated the movement of Divine Mercy in our times. In what ways do people who believe that God is merciful live differently from people who believe that God requires perfection based on following certain rules? What is your image of God, and how is that reflected in the way you live?

_____

_____

_____

_____

_____

2. Lacking the personal gifts for greatness as the world knew it, and limited by her circumstances, Thérèse recognized early on that she would be a "little flower" in God's kingdom. How do your circumstances shape the way you respond to God? Are you resentful or accepting of your circumstances?

_____

_____

_____

_____

_____

3. Thérèse felt that God went before her, preventing her from falling into grave sin. Have you experienced God's "foreseeing love" in your life? When? Did you notice at the time that you were in need of God's grace, or did that become clear only later?

_____

_____

_____

_____

_____

4. It is "the nature of love . . . to humble oneself," Thérèse wrote (SS 14). What challenges do you experience when you know you should humble yourself in a situation but resist doing so? How do you overcome your resistance?

_____

_____

_____

_____

_____

Act!

Guided by Thérèse's insights, how can you let God's mercy take deeper root in your life? Will you allow his mercy to change you?

Session 3

THE SPIRITUALITY
OF LITTLENESS

Sacred Scripture

"I will proclaim what has been hidden from the foundation of the world." (Matthew 13:35)

Jesus said, "I thank you, Father, Lord of heaven and earth, because you have hidden these things from the wise and the intelligent and have revealed them to infants."
(Matthew 11:25)

Many waters cannot quench love,
    neither can floods drown it.
If one offered for love
    all the wealth of one's house,
    it would be utterly scorned. (Song of Solomon 8:7)

Whosoever is a little one, let him come to me.
(Proverbs 9:4, DR)

For to him that is little, mercy is granted.
(Wisdom 6:7, DR)

He shall feed his flock like a shepherd: he shall gather together the lambs with his arm, and shall take them up in his bosom.
(Isaiah 40:11, DR)

You shall be carried at the breasts, and upon the knees they
    shall caress you.

As one whom the mother caresseth, so will I comfort you. (Isaiah 66:12-13, DR)

I will not take . . . he goats out of thy flocks.
For all the beasts of the woods are mine. . . .
If I should be hungry, I would not tell thee: for the world is mine, and the fullness thereof.
Shall I eat the flesh of bullocks? or shall I drink the blood of goats?
Offer to God the sacrifice of praise: and pay thy vows to the most High. (Psalm 49:9-10, 12-14, DR)

A Samaritan woman came to draw water, and Jesus said to her, "Give me a drink." (John 4:7)

Words of St. Thérèse

O my dear Sister [Marie]! you ask me to give you a souvenir of my retreat. . . . Since Mother Prioress permits it, it will be a joy for me to come and speak with you who are doubly my Sister, with you who lent me your voice promising in my name that I wished to serve Jesus only. This child [Thérèse herself], dear little godmother, whom you offered to the Lord and who speaks to you this evening, is one who loves you as a child loves its mother. Only in heaven will you understand the gratitude that overflows my heart. O my dear Sister, you wish to hear about the secrets Jesus confides to your little sister; however, I realize He confides these secrets to you too, for you are the one who taught me how to gather the divine instructions.

Nevertheless, I am going to stammer some words even though I feel it is quite impossible for the human tongue to express things which the human heart can hardly understand.

Do not believe I am swimming in consolations; oh, no, my consolation is to have none on earth. Without showing Himself, without making His voice heard, Jesus teaches me in secret; it is not by means of books, for I do not understand what I am reading. Sometimes a word comes to console me, such as this one which I received at the end of prayer (after having remained in silence and aridity): "*Here is the teacher whom I am giving you; he will teach you everything that you must do. I want to make you read in the book of life, wherein is contained the science of LOVE* [words of Our Lord to St. Margaret Mary as quoted in *Little Breviary of the Sacred Heart*]. The science of Love, ah, yes, this word resounds sweetly in the ear of my soul, and I desire only this science. *Having given all my riches for it*, I esteem it as *having given nothing* as did the bride in the sacred Canticles [Song of Solomon]. I understand so well that it is only love which makes us acceptable to God, that this love is the only good I ambition. Jesus deigned to show me the road that leads to this Divine Furnace, and this road is the *surrender* of the little child who sleeps without fear in its Father's arms. "Whoever is a *little one*, let him come to me." So speaks the Holy Spirit through the mouth of Solomon. This same Spirit of Love also says: "*For to him that is little, mercy will be shown.*" The Prophet Isaiah reveals in His name that on the last day: "*God shall feed his flock like a shepherd; he shall gather together the lambs with his arms, and shall take them up in his bosom.*" As though these promises were not sufficient, this same prophet whose gaze was already plunged into the eternal depths cried out in the Lord's name: *"As one whom a mother caresses, so will I comfort you; you shall be carried at the breasts and upon the knees they will caress you."*

After having listened to words such as these, dear godmother, there is nothing to do but to be silent and to weep with gratitude and love. Ah! if all weak and imperfect souls felt what the least of souls feels, that is, the soul of your little Thérèse, not one would despair of reaching the summit of the mount of love. Jesus does not demand great actions from us but simply *surrender* and *gratitude*. Has He not said: *"I will not take the he-goats from out your flocks. . . . . If I were hungry, I would not tell you, for the world is mine. . . . Shall I eat the flesh of bulls or shall I drink the blood of goats? OFFER TO GOD THE SACRIFICES OF PRAISE AND THANKSGIVING."*

See, then, all that Jesus lays claim to from us; He has no need of our words but only of our *love*, for the same God who declares He *has no need to tell us when He is hungry* did not fear *to beg* for a little water from the Samaritan woman. He was thirsty. But when He said: *"Give me to drink,"* it was the *love* of His poor creature the Creator of the universe was seeking. He was thirsty for love. Ah! I feel it more than ever before, Jesus is *parched*, for He meets only the ungrateful and indifferent among His disciples in the world, and among *His own disciples,* alas He finds few hearts who surrender to Him without reservations, who understand the real tenderness of His infinite Love.

—*Story of a Soul,* 187–89

Consider!

Thérèse wrote these words to help her sister Marie under-stand the scriptural foundation of the little way. Marie was thirteen years older than Thérèse and had entered Carmel two years before Thérèse. As a sister in the Carmelite community, Thérèse could rightly call Marie "doubly my Sister." Marie was also Thérèse's godmother and had counseled her during her teenage scrupulosity.

During their seven years in the community together, Marie had admired her little sister's growth in self-confidence and spiritual wisdom. Marie also recognized that, at this time, Thérèse's death was imminent, and she asked her during her personal retreat to write a clarification of her "*little doctrine*" of holiness, her "little way"—"the secrets Jesus confides" to her.

Thérèse had begun to suffer the symptoms of tuberculosis about six months before Marie's request and knew herself to be dying—she had about a year to live. So even though not physically well and suffering a spiritual "trial of faith," Thérèse accommodated Marie by quickly responding. She wrote a four-teen-page letter to Marie that has become the second section of the current editions of *Story of a Soul*.

Affirming her great respect and love for Marie, Thérèse began her reply to her oldest sister by assuring her that Jesus was con-fiding all the same "secrets" to her that he confided to Thérèse herself. Thérèse was convinced that her little way was not a spe-cial revelation but was available to anyone who contemplated the life and teaching of Jesus and of St. Paul.

The "secrets" that Marie wanted to learn were the secrets of the "science of love," which Thérèse had desired to know from her youth. These secrets are revealed to the "little ones," who are aware of their own spiritual poverty and weakness and know they need God's love and mercy.

From her experience of living in a loving family, and from her practice of charity at home and in Carmel, Thérèse had glimpsed the secret of God's love. In contemplating Jesus' life, she saw that God's love was even vaster and deeper than any human love could be. She saw the fundamental "secret" of Jesus' revelation that God's love is never hostile, coercive, or violent.

Thérèse recognized that human love, however well intentioned, was sometimes poisoned by violence. During her early years, while thinking that she was a loving person, she had been violent not to others but to herself. She had neglected her own courage, compromised her inner freedom, and violated her own integrity and true self by compulsively needing to please others. At that time, she had a blind spot to the self-violence of being in bondage to excessive feelings of needing to please others, and she was overpowered by self-pity and neediness.

When she entered the Carmelite community, she quickly noticed the violence of some well-intentioned sisters who were also enslaved by their feelings. They were bullied by their need to be perfect and tried to bully Thérèse. They corrected her with harshness, attempting to coerce her into becoming a perfect novice.

Thérèse's understanding that God's love is without violence was an essential "secret" that had been "hidden" from the wise by their own arrogance and "hidden from the foundation of the world" by the arrogance and violence of cultures throughout human history. Since all the pagan gods that ancient Israel knew of were violent, the religious and social culture of Israel began to attribute violence to the one true God.

Jesus, however, revealed that the one true God of Israel did not retaliate but willed that all his children love Him, themselves, and one another without violence. This reality, "hidden" before Jesus' life, was at the heart of the "secret" of love that Thérèse taught in her little way and tried to disclose to Marie.

※ ※ ※ ※ ※ ※

Marie had educated Thérèse as a child "to gather the divine instructions." So now Thérèse told Marie that Marie herself also knew, by her contemplation of Jesus, of God's merciful forgiveness and nonviolent love. Marie would recognize God's love even more fully as she continued to contemplate and appreciate her own imperfect life.

Thérèse's awareness of her own personal sinfulness had become the first step on her walking the little way of love. Her second step was her willingness to surrender herself, more and more deeply, to the embrace of God's mercy. With these two steps taken over and over again, Thérèse walked her little way of love, and she invited Marie to do the same. The realization of having been graciously forgiven and welcomed into God's love empowered Thérèse, even impelled her, to extend to herself and others the same forgiving, nonviolent way God had shared with her.

The words of Proverbs, "Whoever is a little one, let him come to me," and of Wisdom, "To him that is little, mercy will be shown," were words of the Holy Spirit that delighted Thérèse and confirmed her way. She was further grateful for the divine teaching of the prophet Isaiah, revealing that God would feed his flock as does a shepherd, gathering the lambs in his arms, taking "them up in his bosom." And if that were not enough, Thérèse was elated to contemplate Isaiah's vision that "as one whom a mother caresses, so will I comfort you; you shall be carried at the breasts and upon the knees they will caress you."

These inspired words gave Thérèse confidence in her "little way" and supported her image of the two steps of her way: accepting her inadequacies and willingly abandoning herself into God's arms, like a child. As she read these passages, all she could do was "be silent and . . . weep with gratitude and love."

Also inspiring Thérèse were the sacred words of the Song of Solomon, and she told Marie that "only love makes us acceptable to God." Thérèse recognized that God accepted her as she loved *all* that God loves, including loving herself while being charitable to others, even enemies, in the same forgiving *way* that God loves.

Thérèse was trying to encourage Marie not to despise herself or violate her own courage but to live in the willingness to acknowledge and repent of her failings. In this way, she would receive God's love in her present spiritual weakness and "littleness." What makes us acceptable to God is living with the mind of Christ, in patience and forgiving love.

Thérèse experienced the spiritual littleness that needed help to rise above her sinful tendencies. She believed that she would enter eternal life, not with the credentials of being perfect or with any great spiritual achievements, but only by being carried in the arms of God. "Jesus does not demand great actions from us," Thérèse told her sister, "but simply *surrender* and *gratitude*"—surrender into God's love and gratitude for who we are at the present moment.

Thérèse knew what it was like to be grateful for being herself and to "*surrender* as the little child who sleeps without fear in its Father's arms." She had done this as an imperfect child in the home of her own loving parents.

Thérèse believed that her spirit of surrender and gratitude to God's love allowed her both to endure the pain of being imperfect and also to render to God "the SACRIFICES OF PRAISE AND THANKSGIVING." These sacrifices, praising and delighting God's heart, were the inner sufferings required to love the way God loves with patience and mercy, without retaliation to herself or others. As she willingly accepted those required sacrifices, Thérèse moved closer and closer to the Source of Love.

For Thérèse, appropriate sacrifices and penances were expressions not of masochism but of willingness to embrace the pain of loving difficult people and of problematic circumstances.

Referring to her attitude during the three months before entering Carmel, Thérèse remarked, "I made a resolution to give myself up more than ever to a *serious* and *mortified* life." She then quickly added, "When I say mortified, this is not to give the impression that I performed acts of penance. Alas, I *never made any*. Far from resembling beautiful souls who practiced every kind of mortification from their childhood, I had no attraction for this. Undoubtedly this stemmed from my cowardliness," she said lightly, "for I could have, like Céline [her younger sister], found a thousand ways of making myself suffer. . . . My mortifications consisted in breaking my will, always so ready to impose itself on others, in holding back a reply, in rendering little services without any recognition" (SS 143).

Thérèse's mortifications and penances were primarily the self-discipline required to be a less self-centered and more loving person. "Offering up" to God the self-inflicted pain of asceticism was common in the spirituality of the time and appealed to the sisters in Carmel. But Thérèse recognized the possible ego promotion in such practices and avoided them.

While obediently participating in the common penitential practices of the community, she had also added some private mortifications during those early days in Carmel. She ended these personal penances, however, when they damaged her health. She was confident that Jesus had no desire that she ruin the gift of being healthy. She knew that God did not need appeasement and that Jesus had come that we may have life and have it to the full (see John 10:10).

Jesus' own approach to suffering was not about desiring pain, she believed, but about desiring to love even if loving required suffering. She moved her asceticism inside, to managing her feelings and will, so that she could live in the spirit of Jesus, who loved without violence to himself or to anyone (see WLW 117ff, 223ff).

Thérèse also understood that God could get things done without work projects from her, unless the work was an expression of her heart work of patience and kindness. Work projects that arose spontaneously from Thérèse's willing surrender and gratitude to God were what God was asking.

When Jesus asked the Samaritan woman for a drink of water, Thérèse believed, he expressed God's longing to be loved the way he himself loved. Thérèse saw that Jesus, like his Father, thirsted for gratitude and the self-surrender of those who accepted and practiced the "real tenderness of His infinite Love" (SS 189).

Jesus desired, she believed, the heart work of welcoming God's love gratefully and the self-sacrifice of sharing God's love in works of charity. The actions that sprang freely from a heart that gratefully accepted God's mercy and that willingly surrendered to God's providence at each moment, *those acts*, Thérèse believed, quenched Jesus' thirst for love.

Especially in her dying, Thérèse came to recognize that her only offering to God was her grateful desire to be more and more united with God and her faith-filled surrender to God's mercy. She had no great accomplishments, neither great prayer experiences nor exceptional penitential practices, nor a store of merit nor spiritual achievements of virtue. In dying Thérèse said she went to God in "confidence and love" (SS 259). That's what it meant for Thérèse to be little and to abandon herself without fear into the Father's arms.

These were the hidden "secrets" of love that Thérèse shared with Marie.

Understand!

1. In what scriptural texts can you find validation for Thérèse's belief that God desires love, not rigid severity and life-demeaning sacrifices?

_____

_____

_____

_____

_____

2. Thérèse, citing the psalmist (see Psalm 50:14), tells us to offer God "sacrifices of praise and thanksgiving." In what ways do praise and thanksgiving soften our hearts to receive God's word or to love our neighbors, especially those who annoy us? Why do you think Thérèse placed such emphasis on praise and gratitude?

_____

_____

_____

_____

_____

3. Jesus thanked the Father for hiding great things from the wise and revealing them to infants (see Matthew 11:25). Keeping Thérèse's experiences in mind, what biblical passages and stories speak to you about the importance of simplicity of heart in seeking God?

_____

_____

_____

_____

_____

4. "Give me a drink," Jesus said to the Samaritan woman (John 4:10). What was he really asking her for? What does this passage reveal to us about God's nature and his own longings? Why do you think Thérèse found this passage so inspiring?

_____

_____

_____

_____

_____

Reflect!

1. Thérèse didn't receive visions or mystical experiences in prayer, and her prayer life was frequently dry. She did receive insights and courage, however, prompting her to be more loving and less impatient. In what ways are your experiences in prayer similar to hers?

_____

_____

_____

_____

2. Prayerful reflection on her life revealed to Thérèse important spiritual truths. What are some truths you have learned from prayerfully reminiscing about your life? In what ways have these insights helped you to change?

_____

_____

_____

_____

_____

3. Thérèse considered that the first step of the spiritual journey was recognizing her own sinfulness. Some spiritual teachers see the first step as being grateful for our giftedness. Which of these two images of the first step have you found more important to your own spiritual growth?

_____

_____

_____

_____

_____

4. How could you put into practice in your life Thérèse's insight that "Jesus does not demand great actions from us but simply *surrender* and *gratitude*" (SS 188)?

_____

_____

_____

_____

_____

Act!

As you enter into a deeper understanding of Thérèse's spirituality, consider the ways in which you do violence to yourself, including all harsh self-talk. Ask the Holy Spirit to guide you away from self-violence to healthy self-love.

Session 4

LOVE YOUR ENEMY

Sacred Scripture

You have heard that it was said, "You shall love your neighbor and hate your enemy." But I say to you, Love your enemies and pray for those who persecute you, so that you may be children of your Father in heaven; for he makes his sun rise on the evil and on the good, and sends rain on the righteous and on the unrighteous. For if you love those who love you, what reward do you have? Do not even the tax collectors do the same? And if you greet only your brothers and sisters, what more are you doing than others? Do not even the Gentiles do the same? Be perfect, therefore, as your heavenly Father is perfect. (Matthew 5:43-49)

But I say to you that listen, Love your enemies, do good to those who hate you, bless those who curse you, pray for those who abuse you. . . .

If you love those who love you, what credit is that to you? For even sinners love those who love them. If you do good to those who do good to you, what credit is that to you? For even sinners do the same. . . . But love your enemies, do good, . . . and you will be children of the Most High; for he is kind to the ungrateful and the wicked. Be merciful, just as your Father is merciful. (Luke 6:27-28, 32-33, 35-36)

The good person out of the good treasure of the heart produces good, and the evil person out of evil treasure produces evil; for it is out of the abundance of the heart that the mouth speaks. (Luke 6:45)

Not everyone who says to me, "Lord, Lord," will enter the kingdom of heaven, but only the one who does the will of my Father in heaven. (Matthew 7:21)

[The] second [commandment] is like [the first]: "You shall love your neighbor as yourself." (Matthew 22:39)

For my yoke is easy, and my burden is light. (Matthew 11:30)

I give you a new commandment, that you love one another. Just as I have loved you, you also should love one another. (John 13:34)

I run the way of your commandments,
    for you enlarge my understanding. (Psalm 119:32)

They sing a new song before the throne and before the four living creatures and before the elders. No one could learn that song except the one hundred forty-four thousand who have been redeemed from the earth. (Revelation 14:3)

Words of St. Thérèse

The Lord, in the Gospel, explains in what *His new commandment* consists. He says in St. Matthew: *"You have heard that it was said, 'You shall love your neighbor and hate your enemy.' But I say to you, love your enemies . . . pray for those who persecute you."* No doubt, we don't have any enemies in Carmel, but there are feelings. One feels attracted to this Sister, whereas with regard to another, one would make a long detour in order to avoid meeting her. And so, without even knowing it, she becomes the subject of persecution. Well, Jesus is telling me that it is this Sister who must be loved, she must be prayed for even though her conduct would lead me to believe that she doesn't love me: *"If you love those who love you, what reward will you have? For even sinners love those who love them."* . . .

And it isn't enough to love; we must prove it. We are naturally happy to offer a gift to a friend; we love especially to give surprises; however, this is not charity, for sinners do this too. Here is what Jesus teaches me also: *"Give to EVERYONE who asks of you, and from HIM WHO TAKES AWAY your goods, ask no return."* Giving to all those who *ask* is less sweet than offering oneself by the movement of one's own heart; again, when they ask for something politely, it doesn't cost so much to give, but if, unfortunately, they don't use very delicate words, the soul is immediately up in arms if she is not well founded in charity. She finds a thousand reasons to refuse what is asked of her, and it is only after having convinced the asker of her tactlessness that she will finally give what is asked, and then only *as a favor*; or else she will render a light service which could have been done in one-twentieth of the time that was spent in setting forth her imaginary rights.

Although it is difficult to give to one who asks, it is even more so *to allow one to take what belongs to you, without asking it back*. O Mother, I say it is difficult; I should have said that this *seems* difficult, for *the yoke of the Lord is sweet and light*. When one accepts it, one feels its sweetness immediately, and cries out with the Psalmist: *"I have run the way of your commandments when you enlarged my heart."* It is only charity which can expand my heart. O Jesus, since this sweet flame consumes it, I run with joy in the way of *Your NEW commandment*. I want to run in it until that blessed day when, joining the virginal procession, I shall be able to follow You in the heavenly courts, singing Your NEW *canticle* which must be *Love*.

—*Story of a Soul*, 224–26

I told myself that charity must not consist in feelings but in works; then I set myself to doing for this Sister what I would do for the person I loved the most. Each time I met her I prayed to God for her, offering Him all her virtues and merits. I felt this was pleasing to Jesus, for there is no artist who doesn't love to receive praise for his works, and Jesus, the Artist of souls, is happy when we don't stop at the exterior, but, penetrating into the inner sanctuary where He chooses to dwell, we admire its beauty. I wasn't content simply with praying very much for this Sister who gave me so many struggles, but I took care to render her all the services possible, and when I was tempted to answer her back in a disagreeable manner, I was content with giving her my most friendly smile, and with changing the subject of the conversation.

—*Story of a Soul*, 222–23

The practice of charity, as I have said, dear Mother, was not always so sweet for me, and to prove it to you I am going to recount certain little struggles which will certainly make you smile. For a long time at evening meditation, I was placed in front of a Sister who had a strange habit and I think many lights because she rarely used a book during meditation. This is what I noticed: as soon as this Sister arrived, she began making a strange little noise which resembled the noise one would make when rubbing two shells, one against the other. I was the only one to notice it because I had extremely sensitive hearing (too much so at times). Mother, it would be impossible for me to tell you how much this little noise wearied me. I had a great desire to turn my head and stare at the culprit who was very certainly unaware of her "click." This would be the only way of enlightening her. However, in the bottom of my heart I felt it was much better to suffer this out of love for God and not to cause the Sister any pain. I remained calm, therefore, and tried to unite myself to God and to forget the little noise. Everything was useless. I felt the perspiration inundate me, and I was obliged simply to make a prayer of suffering; however, while suffering, I searched for a way of doing it without annoyance and with peace and joy, at least in the interior of my soul. I tried to love the little noise which was so displeasing; instead of trying not to hear it (impossible), I paid close attention so as to hear it well, as though it were a delightful concert and my prayer (which was not the *Prayer of Quiet*) was spent in offering this concert to Jesus.

—*Story of a Soul,* 249–50

Consider!

"No doubt, we don't have any enemies in Carmel," Thérèse reflected. She knew she was living with women dedicated to

God, trying to be as loving as possible, while struggling with their weaknesses. None of the sisters intended to hurt others or be an enemy. Yet Thérèse herself, especially during her first months in the community, had felt the bullying of some of the sisters. Even the prioress, Mother Gonzague, had been severe with Thérèse, and Mother Gonzague was imitated by some of the sisters who, with good intentions but with harshness, attempted to help Thérèse obey the community regulations perfectly.

As a young sister, Thérèse, thinking she could like everyone, was disappointed in herself for her vengeful feelings and disappointed in the community for not welcoming her as she expected. Thérèse tried to love the sisters she didn't like but still felt annoyance and antipathy toward some troublesome sisters. She learned that hostility was the natural feeling of being in the presence of the enemy, so to her assessment that "we don't have any enemies in Carmel," Thérèse added honestly and humbly, "but there are feelings."

* * * * * *

A major advance in Thérèse's understanding of the connection between feelings and "the enemy" came after eight years in Carmel, when "her second mother," Pauline, then prioress, was up for reelection.

The opposing candidate and now former prioress, Mother Gonzague, was a strong leader and a very successful fundraiser in her several previous terms of office. Thérèse knew that she was holy in her own way. Toward the end of her life, Thérèse even thanked Mother for not pampering her and so preventing her from becoming the community "pet" or "baby"—a role Thérèse had played at home to her great spiritual harm.

Mother Gonzague was, however, given to gossip and rivalry. She could be impulsive, bullying, vulnerable to criticism; and she held grudges. She sometimes bent community rules to please herself and her favorites.

Under Pauline's leadership, now ending, the rule was applied equally, consistently, and according to custom. Thérèse knew that her older sister was a loving person. She felt certain that Pauline would easily be reelected.

After seven contentious ballots, Pauline lost. Thérèse was devastated.

As Thérèse contemplated her reaction to the election, she saw that the majority of sisters felt threatened by Pauline and so opposed her. Thérèse recognized that these sisters, perceiving Pauline through the interior lens of fear and hostility, made Pauline "the enemy." If they had known Pauline better and felt differently about her, the vote would have been different.

Thérèse began to understand a truth of "the science of love." She recognized that the qualities of her own heart—the lens of her perception and the power of her thoughts and feelings— prompted the way she responded, determining the kind and number of her enemies. The enemy was less an objective reality and more the result of subjective calculations affected by blind spots. If she saw through the lens of faith, and rose above her natural hostile thoughts and fearful feelings, enemies would decrease. How she saw was how she loved and did not love. Both loving and not loving were "inside jobs."

To Jesus' words that "it is out of the abundance of the heart that the mouth speaks" (Luke 6:45), Thérèse could have added,

"And out of the darkness of the heart, the blindness of the mind, and the caprice of the feelings come enemies."

In writing the last two chapters of her memoirs during the final year of her life, Thérèse told several stories of how she coped with being in the presence of an "enemy"—the stories of being splashed with laundry water by a thoughtless sister, of trying unsuccessfully to please an older, grouchy sister, and of enduring the disturbing sound of the sister behind her in chapel. The stories disclose the qualities within Thérèse's heart that helped her establish the lens of faith. They are stories of how she managed the "inside job" of seeing in the spirit of faith, responding to hurt without fear or defensiveness, and rising above natural feelings of hostility. They are, in fact, parables of how any person might fulfill the gospel call to "love the enemy."

Thérèse reflected on Jesus' words: *If you love those who love you, what reward will you have? For even sinners love those who love them.* Love was not a matter of "I like you because you like me." Authentic love, Thérèse understood, came from the decision of her heart, committed to loving even those she did not like and those who did not like her. God loved inclusively, "the just and the unjust," even those who chose to be his enemies.

The sister who sat behind Thérèse in the chapel making a disrespectful and nerve-racking noise seemed to qualify as "the enemy." Thérèse did not call her that but referred to her equivalently as "the culprit."

The sound the sister made unconsciously was driving Thérèse to feelings of irritation and antagonism. She was in the presence of the enemy. Her natural feelings of retaliating prompted thoughts of turning and giving the sister a dirty look. Thérèse was sure that a hostile glance would stop the noise, but she quickly recognized that it would not be the loving thing to do.

Thérèse did not reject or ignore her vengeful feelings; neither did she fight the sister. Rather, by praying to see with the eyes of faith, from God's point of view, Thérèse adjusted her vision and surrendered her natural expectations. Maintaining her inner freedom, she willingly endured her angry feelings, slowly dissolving them in prayer. She was finally able to respond creatively and compassionately to the situation.

She even tried to "love the little noise which was so displeasing," but of course, that proved impossible. So then she "paid close attention so as to hear it well, as though it were a delightful concert and my prayer (which was not the *Prayer of Quiet*) was spent in offering this concert to Jesus" (SS 250).

Without retaliating and without doing emotional violence to herself or to the sister, Thérèse, by prayer and faith, successfully fulfilled Jesus' call to "love the enemy."

Thérèse learned she could use this same inner process of dissolving her hostile feelings and loving the enemy when having the responsibility for correcting a person or changing a situation. Immediately after Mother Gonzague had won the election, she asked Thérèse to continue to teach the newer community members. In that capacity, Thérèse's spirit of faith cultivated the heart qualities of love that had saved her from reacting with hostility to "the culprit" in the chapel or with harshness to the new sisters' mistakes. And so she avoided the bullying some of the community had inflicted on her for her early blunders.

Thérèse's faith vision grounded her inner freedom, freeing her from taking personally the sisters' faults and preventing her from being bullied by her own feelings. Responding compassionately, meeting each sister on the sister's own terms, she corrected creatively, flexibly, and without holding to her preferences or expectations. To one sister she was firm, to another more lenient; to one she was very serious, to another humorous.

What she could not change without bullying the sisters or without willfully imposing her own agenda, she saw as best left to God's providence. In prayer she abandoned herself to God's will, grateful for the often hidden grace of the present moment and thankful for the sisters' goodwill.

Responding to the new sisters, Thérèse saw more clearly the inner qualities she needed in order to act in a loving way. She recognized that the "inside job" of love was possible only with the heart qualities of inner freedom, compassion, creativity, and self-abandonment to God with gratitude—all in a spirit of willingness and not in an attitude of willfulness or bullying of herself or others.

✻ ✻ ✻ ✻ ✻ ✻

Thérèse also came to know another dimension of the "science of love"—the practical side. "Charity," she wrote, "must . . . consist . . . in works," not just in words or prayers (SS 222).

Thérèse quickly recognized that the proof of love was not simply the work of giving gifts to friends. As a child, she had given little favors with strings attached and so without inner freedom. Her good works had been poisoned by excessive feelings of needing to please, to be admired, and to feel good about herself. She acted from codependency.

To give to friends was no proof of love, but to "*Give to EVERYONE who asks of you, and from HIM WHO TAKES AWAY your goods, ask no return*"—yes, to do *that* would be proof of love, especially, Thérèse knew, if the request came with rudeness. If she could be free within, not dominated by hostile feelings and not "immediately up in arms,"and if she could respond with the heart qualities of love—then she could love authentically. Inner freedom, compassion, creativity, the willingness to not bully herself or others, abandonment to God's will, and a grateful-to-God response to an impolite request could only come from a heart "well founded in charity" (see WLW 212).

If, however, Thérèse found a "thousand reasons to refuse what is asked of her" and then granted the request with resentment, only after she had shamed the sister by pointing out her rudeness, *that* would be a kind of retaliation, a form of emotional violence, and clearly not an act of love. Nor would it be loving if Thérèse responded to a request with condescension, "as a favor," or if she required her "imaginary rights" to be honored by making a big unnecessary fuss over "a light service."

Thérèse was writing these pages for Mother Gonzague, so now she directly addressed the superior. "O Mother," she wrote, "I say it is difficult [to love]; I should have said that this *seems* difficult, for *the yoke of the Lord is sweet and light.*" Thérèse had noted that her own personal best proof of love was her willingness to give even without asking anything back. Responding generously in that willing way, Thérèse knew, dealt a death blow to her ego's neediness to be pleasing and admired. Now she was subtly suggesting that giving without standing on a pedestal would also challenge Mother Gonzague's way of trying to be loving.

By addressing Mother Gonzague, Thérèse appears to be discretely asking her to accept a gift—the gift of Thérèse's reflections on her own struggles to love. Thérèse seemed to hope that, by her self-disclosure, she would prompt Mother Gonzague to reflect on her own fumbling way of dealing with her sister favorites and sister enemies. Thérèse had learned from her early encounters with Mother Gonzague that the superior could be impulsively harsh in her clumsy efforts to love with firmness. Now Thérèse was loving Mother Gonzague with gentleness by sharing her insights and challenging the superior to love more freely, kindly, and inclusively, confident that "the yoke of the Lord is sweet and light." If Mother Gonzague could bear the pain of not being so full of herself, she would be able to cry "out with the Psalmist: '*I have run the way of your commandments when you [God] enlarged my heart.*'"

Thérèse ends her reflections with the prayer "O Jesus, since this sweet flame [of love] consumes it [the heart], I run with joy in the way of *Your NEW commandment*. I want to run in it until that blessed day when, joining the virginal procession, I shall be able to follow You in the heavenly courts, singing Your NEW *canticle* which must be *Love*" (SS 226). Thérèse wanted to join with Mother Gonzague in the "virginal procession" and "sing a new song before the throne" of God in the heavenly courts (see Revelation 14:3).

Understand!

1. Can you identify occasions in his daily life when Jesus lived in a way that was loving to his enemy or those who were hostile to him, without retaliation for slights or injustices?

_____

_____

_____

_____

_____

_____

2. Although it's been said that "feelings are neither good nor bad but just are," Thérèse thought that some feelings—like hostility, rivalry, and retaliation—were not good. What are some Scripture passages that would support her belief? Do you agree with her understanding?

_____

_____

_____

_____

_____

3. Why do you think Jesus describes his yoke as easy and himself as gentle (see Matthew 11:28-30)? How is his gentleness revealed in his interactions with others? In what ways do you think this passage might have helped Thérèse as she pursued her little way?

_____

_____

_____

_____

_____

4. Jesus said to "pray for those who persecute you" (Matthew 5:44). Thérèse applied this teaching to those sisters she found difficult or who seemed to dislike her. How does this passage and similar passages about God's mercy help you when you find yourself in challenging circumstances?

_____

_____

_____

_____

_____

Reflect!

1. How have you dealt with hostile feelings and managed to love those you do not like or who do not like you? In what ways have you experienced emotional violence either from within or from other people?

_____

_____

_____

_____

_____

2. Thérèse managed her feelings as a significant lifelong spiritual self-discipline. How have you experienced the connection between managing your feelings and practicing virtue?

_____

_____

_____

_____

_____

3. How would you explain Thérèse's little way to someone who wants to love the enemy and themselves authentically, as Thérèse did, but does not want to be a doormat? What are some ways you have been able to "love your enemy" while maintaining your boundaries and loving yourself?

_____

_____

_____

_____

_____

4. In the story of the annoying sister in chapel, did Thérèse implement the six heart qualities of love? Which ones? Have you noticed yourself implementing one or all of these same qualities when you acted in a loving way?

_____

_____

_____

_____

_____

Act!

Which of Thérèse's ideas or actions regarding love could you implement with spiritual profit right now? Choose one, and begin to incorporate it into your daily life.

Session 5

THE STORY OF ZACCHAEUS

Sacred Scripture

He entered Jericho. . . . A man was there named Zacchaeus; he was a chief tax collector and was rich. He was trying to see who Jesus was, but on account of the crowd he could not, because he was short in stature. So he ran ahead and climbed a sycamore tree to see him, because he was going to pass that way. When Jesus came to the place, he looked up and said to him, "Zacchaeus, hurry and come down; for I must stay at your house today." So he hurried down and was happy to welcome him. All who saw it began to grumble and said, "He has gone to be the guest of one who is a sinner." Zacchaeus stood there and said to the Lord, "Look, half of my possessions, Lord, I will give to the poor; and if I have defrauded anyone of anything, I will pay back four times as much." Then Jesus said to him, "Today salvation has come to this house, because he too is a son of Abraham. For the Son of Man came to seek out and to save the lost." (Luke 19:1-10)

Despised, and the most abject of men, a man of sorrows, and acquainted with infirmity: and his look [face] was as it were hidden and despised, whereupon we esteemed him not. (Isaiah 53:3, DR)

At three o'clock Jesus cried out with a loud voice, . . . "My God, my God, why have you forsaken me?" (Mark 15:34)

"Will the Lord spurn forever,
and never again be favorable?

Has his steadfast love ceased forever?
Are his promises at an end for all time?" (Psalm 77:7-9)

And Jesus said to him, "Foxes have holes, and birds of the air have nests; but the Son of Man has nowhere to lay his head." (Matthew 8:20)

[Jesus said,] "But when you give alms, do not let your left hand know what your right hand is doing." (Matthew 6:3)

And Mary said,
"My soul magnifies the Lord,
    and my spirit rejoices in God my Savior,
for he has looked with favor on the lowliness of his servant.
    Surely, from now on all generations will call me blessed;
for the Mighty One has done great things for me,
        and holy is his name." (Luke 1:46-49)

Words of St. Thérèse

Dear Céline,
. . . Jesus has attracted us together. . . . He has raised us above all the fragile things of this world whose image passes away. He has placed, so to speak, *all things* under our feet. Like Zacchaeus, we climbed a tree to see Jesus. . . . And now what science is He about to teach us? Has He not taught us all? . . . Let us listen to what He is saying to us: "Make haste to descend, I must lodge today at your house." Well, Jesus tells us to descend. . . . Where, then, must we descend? Céline, you

know better than I, however, let me tell you where we must now follow Jesus.

In days gone by, the Jews asked our divine Savior: "Master, where do you live?" And He answered: "The foxes have their lairs, the birds of heaven their nests, but I have no place to rest my head."

This is where we must descend in order that we may serve as an abode for Jesus. To be so poor that we do not have a place to rest our head. This is, dear Céline, what Jesus has done in my soul during my retreat. . . . You understand, there is question here of the interior. Besides, has not the exterior already been reduced to nothing by means of the very sad trial of Caen? . . .

In our dear Father, Jesus has stricken us in the most sensitive exterior part of our heart; now let us allow Him to act, He can complete His work in our souls. . . .

What Jesus desires is that we receive Him into our hearts. No doubt, they are already empty of creatures, but, alas, I feel mine is not entirely empty of myself, and it is for this reason that Jesus tells me to descend. . . .

He, the King of kings, humbled Himself in such a way that His face was hidden, and no one recognized Him, . . . and I, too, want to hide my face, I want my Beloved alone to see it, that He be the only one to count my tears, . . . that in my heart at least He may rest His dear head and feel that there He is known and understood!

—*General Correspondence,* 761–62

Consider!

Thérèse wrote this letter to encourage Céline, who was caring for their seriously ill father at home. Immediately after Thérèse had left home to enter the convent, their father suffered a series of strokes and began hallucinating. On one occasion, he disappeared for several days, only to be found wandering in a nearby town. At another time, he acquired a gun to protect Céline.

At the time that Thérèse wrote to Céline, their father had returned home after more than three years of confinement in an asylum for the mentally ill in the town of Caen. During his last painful visit to Carmel to see his daughters, he covered his head and face and spoke incoherently. He could make only a pitiful gesture, whispering, "In heaven." Thérèse wept copious tears.

Their father's suffering was distressing to both Céline and Thérèse as they helplessly, desperately watched their father's agonizing descent into the dark, forbidding world of the mentally ill. Adding to Thérèse's anguish were rumors circulating in the town and becoming part of the gossip in the Carmelite community, blaming her father's insanity on Thérèse's leaving home.

Thérèse, who thought she could bear even more in her early sufferings of living community life, now believed she had reached the limit of her endurance. Her only consolation was to have faith that this suffering was God's transformative work in her and in Céline. She prayed that they would be able to persevere.

The completion of God's work in Thérèse's soul began when she came to recognize, in her father's distraught countenance, the bleeding, hidden face of Jesus in his passion. Pauline had directed Thérèse's piety as a child to the Hidden Face of Jesus; now Thérèse made that devotion the most important emphasis of her contemplation. Thérèse was consoled knowing that her father was participating in the suffering of Jesus Christ, who emptied himself for all the world.

Thérèse desired to hide her face too and be seen only by God. She wished that only God would know her pain and that in her heart Jesus could find a home, lay his head, and feel understood in his suffering.

Within a year, Thérèse had added "the Hidden Face" to her name. Henceforth she would be known as Sister Thérèse of the Child Jesus and the Hidden Face.

Her father's illness was the first real challenge to Thérèse's faith in God's love. Her spiritual anguish resonated with Jesus' agony and with the distress of the psalmist: "What science [of love] is Jesus about to teach us?" Thérèse wondered. "Well, Jesus tells us to descend." In her heart, Thérèse questioned where God was in the innocent sufferings of her saintly, beloved father. She could not answer her own torment until her heart was purified by the suffering, which deepened her awareness of how God loved her in her pain and how in pain she could respond to God's love.

The year after Thérèse entered Carmel, and before her father began his "descent," she had written of her great ambition to love God: "I would so much like to love Him! Love Him more than He has ever been loved!" (GC 500). But now Thérèse opened her heart to a richer awareness of how she could love God.

"Jesus tells us to descend" (GC 761), she said. Thérèse recognized that Jesus was asking her in her suffering "to come down," to empty herself, so that he could find a place of repose, filling her liberated heart with his love.

The Carmelite lifestyle had already freed and emptied Thérèse of creatures, but she saw that she was not empty of her self-centered ambitions, particularly to be God's greatest lover. She was enlightened by her reading of John of the Cross: to ascend, one must descend. The person who loves God renounces not only exterior things but also interior preconceptions, expectations, vain thoughts and feelings, even spiritual ambitions. The loving person finally not only *has nothing* but *is nothing* that God does not want. "You understand," Thérèse told Céline, "there is question here of the interior."

Her identity as a perfect, loving, holy person still occupied space in the deep interior of her heart. To provide an empty heart in which Jesus could find rest, Thérèse would relinquish even her tendency to her willful spiritual ambitions.

Only her willing cooperation with the Holy Spirit, by complete surrender to God's providence—only *that* would provide the spiritual poverty in her heart that would draw God's love. Her willingness would be *her gift of love* for God, and God would fill her emptiness with *his gift of love* for her.

So while continuing to love God by doing God's will and continuing to long to be even more united to her Beloved, she would now willingly empty herself to simply let God's love fill her in her suffering—to let God love her on God's terms. Imitating Jesus' self-surrender, Thérèse let her *love of God* be primarily welcoming God's *love for her,* abandoning herself to God's providence.

* * * * * *

Thérèse's willingness to empty herself, to surrender herself—this did not mean doing nothing. It meant above all accepting the pain required to respond actively to God's will in the present moment. Prayer and faith slowly dissolved Thérèse's willfulness, and her willpower became a willingness to take the proper and difficult initiatives to do acts of charity.

Nor did emptying herself of herself mean neglecting her responsibilities or failing to develop her natural human and spiritual gifts. Approaching her twentieth year, she cultivated, at the request of her superior, creative and artistic skills of writing poetry, painting, design, and stitching. When asked to assist in the formation of the new community members, Thérèse began to use her gift of wisdom to teach creatively and her gift of empathy to correct compassionately. She also developed skills of spiritual counseling as she responded to both older and younger members of the community seeking her advice.

Encouraging the sisters to empty themselves of their egotism, comparisons, and rivalry, Thérèse advised them to reject self-justification, gossip, blaming, and complaining. In spiritual poverty, they could bear patiently one another's idiosyncrasies and not be personally offended and hostile. They could also do little acts of charity inconspicuously and not make a fuss over small services. Nor would they need everything perfect, including themselves.

Doing acts of charity willingly, without fuss or resentment, was one way that Thérèse herself responded to the call to self-emptying. During her early years, creating a fuss seemed to be in her DNA. Then in prayer, she saw a blind spot, the self-centeredness involved in fussing. She noticed that her fussing was ego food, and with nothing to feed on, the ego tended to disappear.

She began to specialize in doing little things and bearing little inconveniences for the sake of being charitable without fussing—to descend and not need to be noticed.

Thérèse had glimpsed the wiles of the ego as early as the age of twelve, when she read about Joan of Arc. At that time, she saw that vanity could poison her desire to imitate Joan's courage and holiness. "When reading the accounts of the patriotic deeds of . . . JOAN of ARC, I had a great desire to imitate them. . . . Then I received . . . one of the greatest graces in my life. . . . I considered that I was born for *glory* . . . [yet not] to perform striking works but to hide [my]self and practice virtue in such a way that the left hand knows not what the right is doing" (SS 72).

Thérèse's great grace was recognizing the subtle relentlessness of the ego and seeing she was called to a life of hidden holiness. Even her desire to be holy and to be God's greatest lover could be disguised ego ambition and not divine inspiration.

At the age of fourteen, Thérèse had a further insight into her need to empty herself when, at her complete Christmas conversion, she found the strength to accept a personal hurt from her father without fuss and instead responded with inconspicuous charity toward him and with authentic love toward herself.

Thérèse's conversion occurred when her father, fatigued after the Christmas midnight Mass, made an offhand remark that pierced the heart of his "little queen." Thérèse, although a teenager, was preparing to play her childish game of pretending to believe in Santa Claus. She was ascending the stairway to her room when her father, annoyed with this annual ritual that helped keep Thérèse the family "baby," whispered to Céline, "Well, fortunately, this will be the last year!" He was not aware that Thérèse overheard his remark.

Even though she felt devastated by her father's criticism, Thérèse did not submit to her usual tearful self-pity nor react violently with accusations against herself or her father. Rather, she bore patiently the pain of feeling rejected by her father and disappointed in herself—a failure at pleasing her father and equally a failure at being perfect.

Grace shining through the wound in Thérèse's pierced heart allowed her to glimpse a blind spot that had grown during the past ten years. Since her mother's death, she had been stumbling along a path of codependency—letting feelings of "extreme touchiness" and fits of weeping dominate her (SS 97). The light of grace revealed what Thérèse had intuitively known: she was engaged in "a terrible fault" that kept her in "the *swaddling clothes of a child*" (SS 97). Suddenly she saw that, in the role of family baby, she was allowing herself to be a victim to the self-violent feelings of neediness, inadequacy, and self-pity. She recognized "in an instant" that she no longer needed those childish feelings. She could stand her ground emotionally and grasp her inner freedom.

Graced with a new awareness and a new courage to surrender herself, she took the next step on the path of authentic love. Experiencing relief and gratitude, she descended the stairs and responded to her father creatively and compassionately, on his terms and not in her neediness. Her authentic joy brought her father back to himself and reawakened his usual enthusiasm (see WLW 39ff; EIG 124ff).

Céline, knowing that Thérèse had heard her father's remark, was amazed and thought she was dreaming when she saw her younger sister's new behavior. Céline was actually witnessing a miracle. Thérèse was a new person (see SS 98).

In the sheer grace of this Christmas conversion, Thérèse glimpsed again the heart qualities that would support and express her love. During the rest of her life, these qualities would slowly grow in her heart: inner freedom, compassion, creativity, willingness to empty herself, self-surrender, and gratitude.

Thérèse had seen the heart qualities in Zacchaeus' heart. She had also previously glimpsed John of the Cross and Teresa of Avila's insight that humility, the foundation of holiness, is the willing acceptance of knowing and bearing one's imperfections, and that humility emerged in the self-abandonment of the loving, trusting heart. She wrote, "What pleases God is that He sees me loving my littleness and my poverty [my imperfections], the blind hope that I have in His mercy" (GC 999).

In this awareness, Thérèse also imitated and praised the Blessed Virgin, who descended into the hidden glory of being loved by God "in her emptiness." In imitating Mary, Thérèse grew in the spirit of "descent," of humility and spiritual poverty. She would let Jesus' love transform her. Gradually, humble self-abandonment became the sole compass of Thérèse's life.

During the final months of her life, Thérèse saw herself more and more in the arms of Mary and more and more like Zacchaeus, being welcomed by Jesus into *his* home. In her dying, Thérèse was completely emptied of herself, and the open space in her heart was filled by God's love. In her final months, she desired more and more to be loved to death by God.

Understand!

1. Jesus revealed both his exterior and interior poverty when he said that the Son of Man had no place to lay his head (see Matthew 8:20). In what specific ways did Jesus, as well as Thérèse, embrace complete poverty, responding to God in total dependence?

_____

_____

_____

_____

_____

2. Isaiah 53 describes the suffering servant of God, shunned and broken yet faithful to the will of God. In what ways do you think this passage helped shape Thérèse in her relationship with God and with other people?

_____

_____

_____

_____

_____

3. Jesus often spoke against hypocrisy and spiritual pride (see, for example, Matthew 6:1). How would you explain Thérèse's insight that religious ambitions might just be disguised ego willfulness with a spiritual name? Has Thérèse's insight helped you in your own spiritual growth?

_____

_____

_____

_____

_____

4. Humility is a key element of faith, a point Jesus makes numerous times in Scripture. Humility is often misunderstood as thinking poorly of yourself. How did Jesus practice and teach authentic humility?

_____

_____

_____

_____

_____

Reflect!

1. How does Jesus' invitation to descend apply to your life?
   What prevents you from responding as spontaneously as did
   Zacchaeus to Jesus' call?

   _____

   _____

   _____

   _____

   _____

2. Do you know a "Zacchaeus," someone who is searching or
   depressed or lonely and needs you to extend an invitation to
   him or her? How could you respond to that need without a
   fuss? How did Thérèse take the initiative with her less lov-
   able sisters in Carmel?

   _____

   _____

   _____

   _____

   _____

3. How does allowing God to love you impact your prayer and life? Describe a particular time in your life when letting God love you was a step in your spiritual growth.

_____

_____

_____

_____

_____

4. Thérèse's Christmas conversion resulted from an overheard chance remark. How has a chance remark helped you to notice a blind spot in your life?

_____

_____

_____

_____

_____

Act!

Thérèse recognized that even her spiritual ambitions could be poisoned by vanity. Take a spiritual inventory, and resolve to root out any tendency toward spiritual pride.

Session 6

THE PARABLE OF THE PHARISEE AND THE TAX COLLECTOR

Sacred Scripture

He also told this parable to some who trusted in themselves that they were righteous and regarded others with contempt: "Two men went up to the temple to pray, one a Pharisee and the other a tax collector. The Pharisee, standing by himself, was praying thus, 'God, I thank you that I am not like other people: thieves, rogues, adulterers, or even like this tax collector. I fast twice a week; I give a tenth of all my income.' But the tax collector, standing far off, would not even look up to heaven, but was beating his breast and saying, 'God, be merciful to me, a sinner!' I tell you, this man went down to his home justified rather than the other." (Luke 18:9-14)

You hypocrites! Isaiah prophesied rightly about you when he said:
   "This people honors me with their lips,
      but their hearts are far from me." (Matthew 15:7-8)

If we say that we have no sin, we deceive ourselves, and the truth is not in us. (1 John 1:8)

The LORD is merciful and gracious,
   slow to anger and abounding in steadfast love. . . .
As a father has compassion for his children,
   so the LORD has compassion for those who fear him.
For he knows how we were made;
   he remembers that we are dust. (Psalm 103:8, 13-14)

Peace I leave with you; my peace I give to you. I do not give to you as the world gives. (John 14:27)

Now all the tax collectors and sinners were coming near to listen to him. And the Pharisees and the scribes were grumbling and saying, "This fellow welcomes sinners and eats with them."

So he told them this parable: "Which one of you, having a hundred sheep and losing one of them, does not leave the ninety-nine in the wilderness and go after the one that is lost until he finds it? When he has found it, he lays it on his shoulders and rejoices. And when he comes home, he calls together his friends and neighbors, saying to them, 'Rejoice with me, for I have found my sheep that was lost.' Just so, I tell you, there will be more joy in heaven over one sinner who repents than over ninety-nine righteous persons who need no repentance.

"Or what woman having ten silver coins, if she loses one of them, does not light a lamp, sweep the house, and search carefully until she finds it? When she has found it, she calls together her friends and neighbors, saying, 'Rejoice with me, for I have found the coin that I had lost.' Just so, I tell you, there is joy in the presence of the angels of God over one sinner who repents." (Luke 15:1-10)

Words of St. Thérèse

[Dear Fr. Bellière,]
. . . I would like to try to make you understand by means of a very simple comparison how much Jesus loves even imperfect souls who confide in Him.

I picture a father who has two children, mischievous and disobedient, and when he comes to punish them, he sees one of them who trembles and gets away from him in terror, having, however, in the bottom of his heart the feeling that he deserves to be punished; and his brother, on the contrary, throws himself into his father's arms, saying that he is sorry for having caused him any trouble, that he loves him, and to prove it he will be good from now on, and if this child asks his father *to punish* him with a *kiss,* I do not believe that the heart of the happy father could resist the filial confidence of his child, whose sincerity and love he knows. He realizes, however, that more than once his son will fall into the same faults, but he is prepared to pardon him always, if his son always takes him by his heart. . . . I say nothing to you about the first child, dear little Brother; you must know whether his father can love him as much and treat him with the same indulgence as the other. . . .

But why speak to you of the life of confidence and love? I explain myself so poorly that I must wait for heaven in order to converse with you about this happy life [of living in confidence and love]. What I wanted to do today was to console you.

—*General Correspondence,* 1153

From Thérèse to Father Roulland:
I know one must be very pure to appear before the God of all Holiness, but I know, too, that the Lord is infinitely just; and it is this justice which frightens so many souls, that is the object of my joy and confidence. . . . I expect as much from God's justice as from His mercy. It is because He is just that "He is compassionate and filled with gentleness, slow to

punish, and abundant in mercy, for He knows our frailty, He remembers we are only dust. As a father has tenderness for his children, so the Lord has compassion on us!!" . . . How would He allow Himself to be overcome in generosity?

. . . At times, when I am reading certain spiritual treatises in which perfection is shown through a thousand obstacles, surrounded by a crowd of illusions, my poor little mind quickly tires; I close the learned book that is breaking my head and drying up my heart, and I take up Holy Scripture. Then all seems luminous to me. . . . [P]erfection seems simple to me, I see it is sufficient to recognize one's nothingness and to abandon oneself as a child into God's arms. Leaving to great souls, to great minds the beautiful books I cannot understand, much less put into practice, I rejoice at being little since children alone and those who resemble them will be admitted to the heavenly banquet. I am very happy there are many mansions in God's kingdom, for if there were only the one whose description and road seem incomprehensible to me, I would not be able to enter there.

—*General Correspondence,* 1093–94

I have only to cast a glance in the Gospels and immediately I breathe in the perfumes of Jesus' life, and I know on which side to run. I don't hasten to the first place but to the last; rather than advance like the Pharisee, I repeat, filled with confidence, the [tax collector's] humble prayer.

—*Story of a Soul,* 258

I've always remained little, . . . having no other occupation but to gather flowers, the flowers of love and sacrifice, and of offering them to God in order to please Him. . . .

There is only one thing to do here on earth: to cast at Jesus the flowers of little sacrifices, to take Him by caresses; this is the way I've taken Him.

—*St. Thérèse of Lisieux: Her Last Conversations,* 139, 257

Consider!

Thérèse wrote her story of the two mischievous children in a letter to Fr. Bellière, a priest for whom she had been assigned to pray. She tried to encourage him to abandon his Jansenistic notion of a wrathful God and imitate the example of the son in her parable who throws himself into his father's arms.

Although Thérèse probably was not thinking specifically of the parable of the Pharisee and the tax collector, her story has similarities to Jesus' story. Both address the same basic issue: since we are sinners, what is the proper orientation of our heart to God? Thérèse saw in Jesus' parable not only two men seeking to pray but two radically different alignments of the errant heart toward God.

The tax collector's heart, in sinfulness, moved toward God, willing to be in a relationship of repentance and love. The Pharisee's heart was equal in sinfulness, but lacking self-awareness, he saw no need to repent and did not desire loving intimacy with God. He rather sought a relationship only of accountability. The tax collector desired to be loved; the Pharisee desired to be distant.

Jesus addressed the parable to "some who trusted in themselves that they were righteous and regarded others with contempt" (Luke 18:9)—almost an exact description of the way the Pharisees are depicted throughout Luke's Gospel. The audiences Jesus intended to address were, no doubt, the "official" Pharisees and those who thought like the Pharisees.

A basic belief of the Pharisees was that moral perfection was the credential of holiness, so Jesus' depiction of the Pharisee's prayer would have captured their attention. They would have confidently anticipated the Pharisee's (and their) victory in this spiritual battle contesting who was the better of the two men.

But everyone hearing Jesus' words would have known from experience that no one is perfect, just as Thérèse knew and heeded the warning of St. John that we must not deceive ourselves about being sinless. Everyone falls; even law-abiding people sometimes honor God only with their lips or their actions, while their hearts are far from him.

The Pharisee could make his prayer only because he lacked the self-knowledge so essential to the humility the tax collector had. Yet to the ears of the listeners, the tax collector's forthright acknowledgment of sinfulness only served to condemn him and confirm the Pharisee's victory. Sinfulness was thought to be a reason to run from God, not to go toward him.

Jesus' final assessment completely upended his audience's anticipation and validated the way of the tax collector: "I tell you," Jesus concluded, "this man went down to his home justified rather than the other" (Luke 18:14). Jesus proclaimed that God did not retaliate against sinners with almighty power and wrathful vengeance. The Father of Jesus welcomed sinners, as Jesus himself did. Jesus taught a new, spiritual way of relating to God. Jesus' teaching is truly shocking.

The Pharisee's prayer was poisoned both by his lack of awareness of his own sinfulness and by his vision of a wrathful, impersonal God who required only perfect law-abiding. Thanking God for his not being like the tax collector, the Pharisee further twisted his heart by establishing an oppositional, violent, condemning relationship with the tax collector.

The Pharisee's prayer, coming from an unaware, self-promoting, and unrepentant heart, was tantamount to running away from himself, from an intimate relationship with God, and from any association with sinful humanity. And he was probably running away in terror, because only love—not separation and not perfect numbers—casts out fear. That is also the attitude and behavior of the first son in Thérèse's story, the son who "gets away" from the father.

The tax collector, however, was not running away from himself, the Pharisee, or God. He loved himself appropriately by focusing his prayer in honest self-awareness. He loved the Pharisee by respecting him and not being his adversary. And he loved God by his sincere willingness to receive God's mercy.

The tax collector's prayer was a cry for help and a desire that God be God in his life—that God be the mercy and love he longed for. This honest, nonviolent, and welcoming orientation of his heart was enough: "This man went down to his home justified" (Luke 18:14).

The message of this parable assured Thérèse that the father in her story could not resist the filial confidence of his son whose heart, like that of the tax collector, was aligned in truth, repentance, and peace. The parable confirmed Thérèse's experience of her own father's love and reminded her again that if a human father loved the repentant child, how much more would that be true of an infinitely loving Father.

* * * * * * *

Struggling to follow the pattern of the Pharisee and discouraged because she was not making much progress in becoming perfect, one young sister came to Thérèse for advice. Thérèse's bold teaching astonished the sister. "Our sins," Thérèse said, "serve to glorify the mercy of God." And even though God knows everything, "There is a science God doesn't know—arithmetic" (TLMT 74–75; see GC 1122).

Thérèse believed that the way *of* God and the way *to* God is the path of love. And love does not keep accounts. The loving God has given *all*, and the loving person gives *all* to God *from* the heart as well as *all in* the heart—all the heart's gifts and imperfections. Jesus welcomed repentant sinners; his priority was not arithmetic. God doesn't count us; he calls us by name.

Thérèse resisted the attitude of the Pharisee and made her own the spirit of the tax collector. She fostered in herself and in the sisters the spirit of self-knowledge, of willing repentance, and of humble trust. "Jesus is teaching her," she wrote of herself, "[not to keep accounts but] to learn 'to draw profit from everything, *from the good* and *the bad* she finds in herself'" (GC 795).

On another occasion, the same sister complained about being unable to be perfectly patient with some of the difficult sisters. "If God wants you to be weak and powerless like a little child," Thérèse asked, "do you think you will be less worthy? Consent, then, to stumble at every step, even to fall, to carry your cross feebly" (TLMT 79).

Thérèse's advice was simple and direct, echoing Jesus' emphasis on loving oneself as well as others. At least be patient with yourself, Thérèse counseled, even though you are not patient with others. Await God's grace, she was advising, prayerfully, patiently, repentantly, and without obsessive shame or guilt.

To another sister, also discouraged in her striving for perfection, Thérèse wrote, "If you are willing to bear serenely the trial of being displeasing to yourself, then you will be . . . [for Jesus] a pleasant place of shelter" (GC 1038). Thérèse was advising the sister to be honest with herself and God. In loving herself in patience and kindness, she would open herself to receive the fullness of God's love (see WLW 181ff; EIG 226ff).

Thérèse returned again and again to emphasize Jesus' priority of the one commandment: love. She advised the sisters to willingly accept their powerlessness, their spiritual poverty, and not hate themselves for being imperfect. Success in virtue, Thérèse taught, is not the point. Love—love of yourself, love of others, and loving trust of God—that is the point.

Thérèse also explained that her little way of imperfection was not a path of irresponsibility or passivity. It was the way of love, and she believed that "a soul that is burning with love cannot remain inactive" (SS 257). Love diffuses itself.

She also knew that overcoming faults required active virtues of patient love of oneself, faith in the power of God, courage, and humility. And further, she experienced the fact that these virtues were attained not so much by willful effort to

overcome imperfection as by the willingness to serenely persevere in active self-awareness, in vigilance, and in a spirit of
prayer and repentance.

As bold as Thérèse's responses to the sisters were, and as dar-
ing in suggesting the depth of God's mercy as her story of the
two sons was, Jesus' parable is even more audacious. The tax
collector was even bolder than the second son in Thérèse's story.
The tax collector acknowledged his sin and asked for gratuitous
mercy. He did not even promise, as the second son did, that "he
will be good from now on."

Of course, in both Jesus' parable and Thérèse's story, the
father knows that his sons will fall often into the same faults,
but God is always loving to the repentant heart that reaches out
"to take Him by caresses" (HLC 257).

❈ ❈ ❈ ❈ ❈ ❈

In Thérèse's day, Catholic spirituality had been contaminated
by Jansenism—a heresy continuing some mistaken inter-
pretations of the Bible that emphasized the need for moral
perfection to appease the wrath and vengefulness of God.
Such false notions of God clouded the Christian religious
imagination, condemning the faithful to a relationship with
God that was fundamentally fearful, rigidly moralistic and
legalistic, and not the relationship Jesus proclaimed—one
essentially trusting, prayerful, and mystical.

In this way, Jansenism basically poisoned the relationship of
intimacy with God that Jesus lived and taught, reducing Christi-
anity to a strictly moralistic religion. When Pope St. John Paul II
proclaimed Thérèse a doctor of the Church, he mentioned quite

explicitly that "she helped to heal souls of the rigors and fears of Jansenism, which tended to stress God's justice rather than his divine mercy" (DAS 8).

Jansenism falsely regarded God's justice as human justice—that is, justice that is vengeful and rejects mercy. From a Jansenistic perspective, human justice, "an eye for an eye" justice (revenge), was the only justice befitting an almighty, wrathful God. But Jesus taught that God is Love, not vengeance, and that God's justice seeks the good of all, providing each in God's household with what each truly needs.

The pope affirmed Thérèse's confidence that God's love and mercy trumped Jansenism and that God's justice is as completely different from human retaliatory, punitive justice as the peace that Jesus gives is different from the peace the world gives (see John 14:27). The pope quoted from Thérèse's teaching: "To me," Thérèse wrote, "He has granted His *infinite Mercy*, and *through it* I contemplate and adore the other divine perfections! All of these perfections appear to be resplendent *with love;* even His justice (and perhaps this even more so than the others) seems to me clothed in *love*" (SS 180; see DAS 8).

Then the pope concluded, "Thus she became a living icon of that God who 'shows his almighty power in his mercy and forgiveness'" (DAS 8). By making Thérèse a doctor of the Church and declaring her an "icon of God," the pope emphasized that Thérèse's life and teaching truly manifest the authentic Christian understanding of God's justice and mercy.

❊ ❊ ❊ ❊ ❊ ❊

Thérèse ends her story of the two sons abruptly, suggesting that Fr. Bellière knows how the father will treat the first child, who "gets away" from the father. That son, Thérèse would have noticed, resembled the lost sheep and the lost coin, all of whom had temporarily "gotten away." Thérèse would have seen that in every case, the rescue came as a complete and underserved gift.

Thérèse invited Fr. Bellière to pray through his feelings of guilt and estrangement from God, encouraging him into a faith vision of confidence and love, certain that God's love does not retaliate but embraces the lost.

Understand!

1. What do you think are the most important teachings in the parable of the Pharisee and tax collector? Can you name any other stories, actions, or instructions in which Jesus reiterates the points he is making in this parable?

_____

_____

_____

_____

_____

2. God's justice "is the object of my joy and confidence," Thérèse said, because his justice fills him with compassion for human frailty (GC 1094; see Psalm 103). In what ways do you think human frailty influences God's justice? How should it influence us when seeking justice from those who have sinned against us?

_____

_____

_____

_____

_____

3. Thérèse said, "Our sins serve to glorify the mercy of God" (TLMT 74). What stories in the Bible demonstrate that sin can ultimately glorify God? What are the possible blessings and risks of Thérèse's statement?

_____

_____

_____

_____

_____

4. Thérèse's story of the two mischievous children and their father captures her own approach to God. How can it help you to approach God in greater freedom?

_____

_____

_____

_____

_____

Reflect!

1. Thérèse finally recognized that "I must bear with myself such as I am with all my imperfections" (SS 207). If you took Thérèse's sentiments to heart, in what ways might you think, feel, and act differently?

_____

_____

_____

_____

_____

2. Have you experienced in your own life the drama of the Pharisee and the tax collector—that is, have you found yourself in the role of one or the other? What insights did you gain from your experience, and how have they helped you to surrender more fully to God?

_____

_____

_____

_____

_____

3. Pope St. John Paul II wrote that Thérèse "helped to heal souls of the rigors and fears of Jansenism, which tended to stress God's justice rather than his divine mercy" (DAS 8). Do you notice traces of Jansenism and perfectionism among Christians in our day? How would you explain God's mercy and truths to a Christian struggling with fear and legalism?

_____

_____

_____

_____

_____

4. Have Jansenism and perfectionism affected your spirituality? Have you ever condemned yourself for certain sins or imperfections and resisted God's mercy? What helped you find the inner freedom to allow God to love and heal you? If you have not found that freedom, where might you start?

_____

_____

_____

_____

_____

Act!

Thérèse advanced in holiness through "the flowers of little sacrifices" that she cast at Jesus' feet (HLC 257). What specific small sacrifices can you make this week that would help you enter into greater interior freedom?

Session 7
MY VOCATION
IS LOVE

Sacred Scripture

Now there are varieties of gifts, but the same Spirit; and there are varieties of services, but the same Lord; and there are varieties of activities, but it is the same God who activates all of them in everyone. To each is given the manifestation of the Spirit for the common good. . . . All [gifts] are activated by one and the same Spirit, who allots to each one individually just as the Spirit chooses.

For just as the body is one and has many members, and all the members of the body, though many, are one body, so it is with Christ. For in the one Spirit we were all baptized into one body. . . .

Indeed, the body does not consist of one member but of many. If the foot would say, "Because I am not a hand, I do not belong to the body," that would not make it any less a part of the body. And if the ear would say, "Because I am not an eye, I do not belong to the body," that would not make it any less a part of the body. If the whole body were an eye, where would the hearing be? If the whole body were hearing, where would the sense of smell be? But as it is, God arranged the members in the body, each one of them, as he chose. If all were a single member, where would the body be? As it is, there are many members, yet one body. The eye cannot say to the hand, "I have no need of you," nor again the head to the feet, "I have no need of you." On the contrary, the members of the body that seem to be weaker are indispensable, and those members of the body that we think less honorable we clothe with greater honor, and our less respectable members are treated with greater respect; whereas our more respectable members do not need this. But God has so arranged the body, . . . that . . . the members may have the same care for one another. If one member suffers, all suffer together with it; if one member is honored, all rejoice together with it.

Now you are the body of Christ and individually members of it. And God has appointed in the church first apostles, second prophets, third teachers. . . . But strive for the greater gifts. And I will show you a still more excellent way.

If I speak in the tongues of mortals and of angels, but do not have love, I am a noisy gong or a clanging cymbal. And if I have prophetic powers, and understand all mysteries and all knowledge, and if I have all faith, so as to remove mountains, but do not have love, I am nothing. If I give away all my possessions, and if I hand over my body so that I may boast, but do not have love, I gain nothing.

Love is patient; love is kind; love is not envious or boastful or arrogant or rude. It does not insist on its own way; it is not irritable or resentful; it does not rejoice in wrongdoing, but rejoices in the truth. It bears all things, believes all things, hopes all things, endures all things.

Love never ends. But as for prophecies, they will come to an end; as for tongues, they will cease; as for knowledge, it will come to an end. For we know only in part, and we prophesy only in part; but when the complete comes, the partial will come to an end. When I was a child, I spoke like a child, I thought like a child, I reasoned like a child; when I became an adult, I put an end to childish ways. For now we see in a mirror, dimly, but then we will see face to face. Now I know only in part; then I will know fully, even as I have been fully known. And now faith, hope, and love abide, these three; and the greatest of these is love. (1 Corinthians 12:4-7, 11-13, 14-28, 31; 13:1-13)

And I, when I am lifted up from the earth, will draw all people to myself. (John 12:32)

In him we live and move and have our being. (Acts 17:28)

No one after lighting a lamp puts it under the bushel basket, but on the lampstand, and it gives light to all in the house. (Matthew 5:15)

Present your bodies as a living sacrifice, holy and acceptable to God, which is your spiritual worship. (Romans 12:1)

What good is it, my brothers and sisters, if you say you have faith but do not have works? Can faith save you? If a brother or sister is naked and lacks daily food, and one of you says to them, "Go in peace; keep warm and eat your fill," and yet you do not supply their bodily needs, what is the good of that? So faith by itself, if it has no works, is dead. (James 2:14-17)

Words of St. Thérèse

During my meditation, my desires caused me a veritable martyrdom, and I opened the Epistles of St. Paul to find some kind of answer. Chapters 12 and 13 of the First Epistle to the Corinthians fell under my eyes. I read there, in the first of these chapters, that *all* cannot be apostles, prophets, doctors, etc., that the Church is composed of different members, and that the eye cannot be the hand *at one and the same time*. The answer was clear, but it did not fulfill my desires and gave me no peace. . . . Without becoming discouraged, I continued my reading, and this sentence consoled me: *"Yet strive after THE BETTER GIFTS, and I point out to you a yet more excellent way."* And the Apostle explains how all *the most PERFECT gifts* are nothing without *LOVE*. That *Charity is the EXCELLENT WAY* that leads most surely to God.

I finally had rest. Considering the mystical body of the Church, I had not recognized myself in any of the members described by St. Paul, or rather I desired to see myself in them *all. Charity* gave me the key to my *vocation*. I understood that if the Church had a body composed of different members, the most necessary and most noble of all could not be lacking to it, and so I understood that the Church *had a Heart and that this Heart was BURNING WITH LOVE. I understood it was Love alone* that made the Church's members act, that if *Love* ever became extinct, apostles would not preach the Gospel and martyrs would not shed their blood. I understood that LOVE COMPRISED ALL VOCATIONS, THAT LOVE WAS EVERYTHING, THAT IT EMBRACED ALL TIMES AND PLACES. . . . IN A WORD, THAT IT WAS ETERNAL!

Then, in the excess of my delirious joy, I cried out: O Jesus, my Love, . . . my *vocation*, at last I have found it. . . . MY VOCATION IS LOVE!

Yes, I have found my place in the Church and it is You, O my God, who have given me this place; in the heart of the Church, my Mother, I shall be *Love*. Thus I shall be everything, and thus my dream will be realized.

Why speak of a delirious joy? No, this expression is not exact, for it was rather the calm and serene peace of the navigator perceiving the beacon which must lead him to the port. . . . O luminous Beacon of love, I know how to reach You, I have found the secret of possessing Your flame.

I am only a child, powerless and weak, and yet it is my weakness that gives me the boldness of offering myself as *VICTIM of Your Love, O Jesus!* In times past, victims, pure and spotless, were the only ones accepted by the Strong and Powerful God. To satisfy Divine *Justice*, perfect victims were necessary, but the *law of Love* has succeeded to the law of fear, and *Love* has chosen me as a holocaust, me, a weak and imperfect creature. Is not this choice worthy of *Love*? Yes, in order that Love be fully satisfied, it is necessary that It lower Itself, and that It lower Itself to nothingness and transform this nothingness into *fire*.

O Jesus, I know it, love is repaid by love alone, and so I searched and I found the way to solace my heart by giving you Love for Love. . . .

Jesus, I cannot fathom the depths of my request; I would be afraid to find myself overwhelmed under the weight of my bold desires. My excuse is that I am a *child*, and children do not reflect on the meaning of their words; however, their parents, once they are placed upon a throne and possess immense treasures, do not hesitate to satisfy the desires of the *little ones*. . . . The heart of a child does not seek riches and glory. . . . She knows only one thing: to love You, O Jesus. . . . [A] *little child*, [she] stays very close to the *throne* of the King and Queen. . . . But how will she prove her *love* since *love* is proved by works? Well, the little child *will strew flowers* . . . that is, not allowing one little sacrifice to escape, not one look, one word, profiting by all the smallest things and doing them through love. I desire to suffer for love.

—Story of a Soul, 193–96

I do not hold in contempt beautiful thoughts . . . ; but for a long time I have understood that we must not depend on them and even make perfection consist in receiving many spiritual lights. The most beautiful thoughts are nothing without good works.

—Story of a Soul, 234

I understand now that charity consists in bearing with the faults of others, in not being surprised at their weakness, in being edified by the smallest acts of virtue we see them practice. But I understood above all that charity must not remain hidden in the bottom of the heart. Jesus has said: *"No one lights a lamp and puts it under a bushel basket, but upon the lamp-stand, so as to give light to ALL in the house."* It seems to me that this lamp represents charity which must enlighten and rejoice not only those who are dearest to us but "ALL *who are in the house"* without distinction.

—Story of a Soul, 220

Lord, I know You don't command the impossible. You know better than I do my weakness and imperfection; You know very well that never would I be able to love my Sisters as You love them, unless *You,* O my Jesus, *loved them in me.* It is because You wanted to give me this grace that You made Your *new* commandment. Oh! how I love this new commandment since it gives me the assurance that Your Will *is to love in me* all those You command me to love!

Yes, I feel it, when I am charitable, it is Jesus alone who is acting in me, and the more united I am to Him, the more also do I love my Sisters.

—Story of a Soul, 221

There is in the Community a Sister who has the faculty of displeasing me in everything, in her ways, her words, her character, everything seems *very disagreeable* to me. And still, she is a holy religious who must be very pleasing to God. Not wishing to give in to the natural antipathy I was experiencing, I told myself that charity must not consist in feelings but in works; then I set myself to doing for this Sister what I would do for the person I loved the most. Each time I met her I prayed to God for her, offering Him all her virtues and merits. I felt this was pleasing to Jesus, for there is no artist who doesn't love to receive praise for his works, and Jesus, the Artist of souls, is happy when we don't stop at the exterior, but, penetrating into the inner sanctuary where He chooses to dwell, we admire its beauty. I wasn't content simply with praying very much for this Sister who gave me so many struggles, but I took care to render her all the services possible, and when I was tempted to answer her back in a disagreeable manner, I was content with giving her my most friendly smile, and with changing the subject of the conversation. . . .

Frequently, when I was at recreation (I mean during the work periods) and had occasion to work with this Sister, I used to run away like a deserter whenever my struggles became too violent. As she was absolutely unaware of my feelings for her, never did she suspect the motives for my conduct and she remained convinced that her character was very pleasing to me. One day at recreation she asked in almost these words: "Would you tell me, Sister Thérèse of the Child Jesus, what attracts you so much toward me; everytime you look at me, I see you smile?" Ah! what attracted me was Jesus hidden in the depths of her soul; Jesus who makes sweet what is most bitter. I answered that I was smiling because I was happy to see her (it is understood that I did not add that this was from a spiritual standpoint).

Dear Mother, I have already told you that my *last means* of not being defeated in combats is desertion; I was already using this means during my novitiate, and it always succeeded perfectly with me.

—*Story of a Soul,* 222–23

Consider!

During the last two years of her life, Thérèse was enthralled by St. Paul's teaching on the mystical body of Christ. She saw that each member needed every other, each having a unique gift to contribute to the fullness of the body. She was inspired to fulfill her desire to know and practice "the science of love" by participating in all the acts of love of all the members of Christ's body. It was a beautiful but impossible desire.

Moreover, she noticed that the lifeblood coursing through the mystical body was God's love, Christ's love, activating all the members to actions of love. In a flash of insight, she understood that by uniting herself with Christ's love, she could support the life of the body and participate in the actions of each member. St. Paul's "more excellent way" of love would be Thérèse's way of fulfilling her bold, beautiful, passionate, impossible desire to share in the good works of all the members of Christ's body.

Further, understanding that if the life force of love dried up, no one would preach the Gospel or live the Christian life, she saw that "LOVE COMPRISED ALL VOCATIONS, THAT LOVE WAS EVERYTHING, THAT IT EMBRACED ALL TIMES AND PLACES."

She also recognized that in heaven her love would continue as a participation in God's love, drawing all creation into the resurrected Christ, at the right hand of the Father. Her love would, then, participate in Love flowing through the Trinity for eternity! Love enveloped all of history, all of time. "IN A WORD, LOVE WAS ETERNAL," she wrote, and she longed to *be* that love.

Thérèse was filled with joy. She had recognized her fundamental vocation within her Carmelite vocation. In her vision of the mystical body of Christ, Thérèse realized the peace of entering into the basic truth of her life and of being capable of fulfilling her primary calling—to be love. "Yes," she declared in delirious joy, "I have found my place in the Church and it is You, O my God, who have given me this place; in the heart of the Church, my Mother, I shall be *Love*."

Realizing the consummation of her only longing, Thérèse was being drawn by a "luminous Beacon of love" into the reality of who she really was—a person who is living and acting and existing in Him who is Love (SS 195; see Acts 17:28).

Thérèse had reached a new and deeper understanding of God's love—the "flame of divine love." In her surge of joy, she also saw the very earthy and immediate application of her new awareness—the flame of divine love was to be extended to "ALL in the house" (SS 220).

If she wished to be love in the heart of the entire Church, she would begin by being love to all in her house, to all the sisters in the community. This she would do by deepening her union with Christ by prayer, by purifying her motives, and especially by performing works of charity. Yet in these very areas of prayer, motivation, and charitable practices, Thérèse had especially experienced her weaknesses and sins.

Thérèse expanded her faith vision. Determining again to imitate the way of the tax collector and the descent of Zaccheus, she would love God by welcoming God into *her* house. She had understood what St. John meant when he wrote, "We love because he first loved us" (1 John 4:19). Having also experienced that "when I am charitable, it is Jesus alone who is acting in me, and the more united I am to Him, the more also do I love my sisters" (SS 221), she saw that "those who say, 'I love God,' and hate their brothers or sisters, are liars" (1 John 4:20).

By first letting God's love find a home in her heart, Thérèse was empowered to love others. Loving God and loving "ALL" in her house were one love. She also understood more clearly that loving herself was not being self-centered but was delighting in God's love of her. Toward the end of her life, she wrote, "God has given me the grace to understand what charity is" (SS 219).

Thérèse was grasping a fundamental reality: there was only one love—God's love.

Her welcoming of God's love flowing to her was "her love of God." Her willingness to be loving was God's love empowering her and was "her love of others." Her simple gratitude, her delight in being embraced by God, was "her love of herself." All love was God's love circulating throughout the mystical body of Christ.

In this vision of being Love at the heart of the Church—participating in this great circle of God's love—she offered herself "as *VICTIM of Your Love, O Jesus!*" Yet how could she fulfill her desire to offer herself to God if, as she had read in the Old Testament, spotless victims alone could be sacrificed to God— and she was not perfect?

In still another spiritual awareness, she saw a solution. In the New Testament, the law of love replaced the law of fear. The Gospel and St. Paul had taught her that God's love is mercy and forgiveness. God did not require satisfaction. Her sacrifice, then, would be enduring the pain of her weakness and embracing, the best she could, any sufferings associated with her acts of charity. She would be a "holocaust" to God's love, not a holocaust to wrath. She would be a "living sacrifice"—living in the loving way of surrendering herself to God's providence, participating in God's love flowing through the mystical body by dying daily to her self-centeredness.

Thérèse was confident that imperfections were no obstacle to God's love in her. She believed that her desire for intimacy with God and her prayer for mercy drew God's mercy. Jesus had come to save those most in need of his mercy. Even and especially in her weaknesses and repentance, God could and would use her as mediator of His own mercy and love to the entire mystical body, to every heart, in every place, and throughout all time.

This mystical and ecstatic vision of love gave Thérèse great joy and consolation, yet she was ever the saint of the practical. She wondered how she would prove her love of Christ, since she believed love is proved by works. She found a solution in her self-image as a spiritually inadequate child.

As a child of God, her primary work was to stay close to her King, in expressions of intimacy and in accepting the little sacrifices required by God's providence. She would therefore not allow any sacrifice, however small, to escape her welcome. In that way, through love for God, without fuss and bitterness, she would profit by doing the smallest act of charity and by enduring every inconvenience.

As an example of her attempt to prove her love, Thérèse told a story of her interactions with a certain particularly annoying sister. This sister displeased Thérèse in just about everything—her looks, her mannerisms, and her character. Thérèse was embarrassingly honest in describing her difficult feelings toward this sister, feelings Thérèse could manage only by deploying the qualities of heart that allowed her to love. These were the qualities she had first glimpsed in the experience of her teenage Christmas conversion and had gradually nurtured into a mature love for her Carmelite sisters.

In some difficult conversations with this particularly troubled and troublesome sister, Thérèse noticed her own tendency to defend herself with emotional violence toward the sister by answering back. At such times, Thérèse quieted herself with a brief prayer, did not take the sister's behavior personally, and regained her inner freedom.

Sensing the sister's own inner pain, Thérèse took a compassionate initiative and responded creatively, in a loving way. She offered the sister a friendly smile and changed the topic. Thérèse was willing to endure the pain of surrendering her own convenience to the patience and kindness that God was asking of her at that moment. It was an example of how Thérèse acted as if the sister were her best friend.

At one point, Thérèse began to notice that sisters who suffered physically were generously cared for, but those suffering emotionally were often ignored. Understanding this, as she grew in compassion and more deliberately extended a loving gesture to this troublesome sister, Thérèse volunteered to work with her. But Thérèse's goodwill was sometimes met with outbursts of rage during the work periods. At such times, all Thérèse could do was flee.

Flight made Thérèse feel as if she were "a deserter," but it was the best she could do at the moment. When she regained her inner freedom, Thérèse returned to the sister in peace. Fleeing was really not deserting; it was a boundary that Thérèse established to protect herself—to love herself while loving the sister.

Thérèse was grateful to God for the ability to respond creatively and compassionately; and the sister never recognized that Thérèse was not her best friend. Thus on one occasion, the sister asked her, "What attracts you so much towards me; everytime you look at me, I see you smile?" (SS 223).

In retrospect, Thérèse could tell this story with some humor, but at the time she suffered intensely. She had to be patient with her hostile feelings toward the sister and her feelings of disappointment in herself.

This is a story filled with irony about Thérèse herself, who desired to be Love at the heart of the Church and yet sometimes struggled to be Love at the heart of her community. At the end of her life, however, Thérèse was described by her novice mistress: "She was an angel of peace for everybody"—a beacon of peace and a flame of Love for ALL in the community (STL 207).

* * * * * *

Thérèse's vision of being Love at the heart of the Church was a bold desire, and it was also a disturbing vision and ambition. Was this the vision and desire of a "little soul," or was it the fantasy of a pompous, self-promoting romantic? Was this a humble expression of God's gifts in her, as she promised to describe in the opening paragraphs of her memories, or the exaggerations of dreamy self-centeredness? Was it another disguised ambition of the ego?

Even as she believed God would use her, imperfect as she was, for God's glory, Thérèse expressed her fear of being overwhelmed by these concerns—"the weight" of her bold desires. She prayed again in confidence, believing that this desire came from the spiritual poverty of a child in the arms of God. She knew, however, that even the heart of a child is not immune to the poison of self-promotion.Therefore, while embracing the unself-consciousness of the child, she added the practical wisdom of the mature woman: she intensified her prayer and her focus on the heart qualities of love. Only in this way could Thérèse successfully walk her little way of love, accepting the truth of her imperfections together with the reality of being immensely blessed by God, called to be Love at the heart of the Church.

Throughout her life, in her everyday faith vision of her role in the mystical body—her "everyday mysticism"—Thérèse walked the very narrow path of humility and faith, avoiding any violence to herself or others. By rejecting and dissolving any thoughts or feelings toward violence, she stayed on her little way of love.

Understand!

1. "The most beautiful thoughts are nothing without good works," Thérèse said (SS 234). In what ways do you think her statement complements St. Paul's emphasis on love in 1 Corinthians 13? What aspects of Paul's "beautiful thoughts" have particular resonance with Thérèse's little way?

_____

_____

_____

_____

_____

2. Thérèse was certain that God "cannot inspire unrealizable desires" (SS 207). Which Scripture passages encourage you to be persistent as you pray for and pursue seemingly impossible desires or situations in your walk of faith?

_____

_____

_____

_____

_____

3. Jesus said that no one lights a lamp and hides it under a bushel basket. Thérèse agreed, saying that love must not be hidden in "the bottom of the heart" (SS 220). How do you reconcile Thérèse's emphasis on hidden sacrifices with Jesus' call to let others "see your good works"? (Matthew 5:16).

_____

_____

_____

_____

_____

4. Scripture speaks often of suffering. What passages help you understand that Thérèse's "desire to suffer for love" (SS 196) was in line with Scripture and not masochistic?

_____

_____

_____

_____

_____

Reflect!

1. What would it mean for you to participate in Thérèse's bold desire to be Love at the heart of the Church?

_____

_____

_____

_____

_____

2. Thérèse was born into a loving family. In what ways do you think this gave her an advantage in being a loving person? What might have been God's providence in giving Thérèse such an advantage? Do you think that, in some providential way, everyone has a unique advantage for his or her mission? If so, what is yours?

_____

_____

_____

_____

_____

3. Thérèse's faith vision is sometimes trivialized by the suggestion that she did only little things. How is Thérèse's emphasis on inconspicuous good works and small sacrifices not trivial?

_____

_____

_____

_____

_____

4. How have you successfully used Thérèse's practice of letting a kind act diffuse a difficult situation?

_____

_____

_____

_____

_____

Act!

Thérèse is regarded as a mystic—not an extraordinary mystic with visions and miracles, but an everyday mystic who put love "on the ground." How does Thérèse invite you to love in concrete, practical ways today?

Session 8

JESUS, DRAW ME

Sacred Scripture

It is no longer I who live, but it is Christ who lives in me. (Galatians 2:20)

Draw me: we will run after thee to the odour of thy ointments. (Song of Solomon 1:3, DR)

Let the same mind be in you that was in Christ Jesus,
   who, though he was in the form of God,
      did not regard equality with God
      as something to be exploited,
   but emptied himself. . . .
      He humbled himself
      and became obedient to the point of death—
      even death on a cross. (Philippians 2:5-7, 8)

The Father will give you whatever you ask him in my name. (John 15:16)

I am now rejoicing in my sufferings for your sake, and in my flesh I am completing what is lacking in Christ's afflictions for the sake of his body, that is, the church. (Colossians 1:24)

Words of St. Thérèse

For me, *prayer* is an aspiration [a surge] of the heart; it is a simple glance directed to heaven, it is a cry of gratitude [recognition] and love in the midst of [embracing] trial as well as joy.

—Story of a Soul, 242; see CCC 2558

Since I have two brothers and my little Sisters, the novices, if I wanted to ask for each soul what each one needed and go into detail about it, the days would not be long enough and I fear I would forget something important. For simple souls there must be no complicated ways; as I am of their number, one morning during my thanksgiving, Jesus gave me a simple means of accomplishing my mission.

He made me understand these words of the Canticle of Canticles: "*DRAW ME, WE SHALL RUN after you in the* [*fragrance*] *of your ointments.*" O Jesus, it is not even necessary to say: "*When drawing me, draw the souls whom I love!*" This simple statement: "*Draw me*" suffices; I understand, Lord, that when a soul allows herself to be captivated by *the* [*fragrance*] *of your ointments*, she cannot run alone, all the souls whom she loves follow in her train; this is done without constraint, without effort; it is a natural consequence of her attraction for You. Just as a torrent, throwing itself with impetuosity into the ocean, drags after it everything it encounters in its passage, in the same way, O Jesus, the soul who plunges into the shoreless ocean of Your Love draws with her all the treasures she possesses. Lord, You know it, I have no other treasures than the souls it has pleased You to unite to mine.

—Story of a Soul, 254

Mother, I think it is necessary to give a few more explanations on the passage in the Canticle of Canticles, *"Draw me, we shall run,"* for what I wanted to say appears to me little understood. *"No man can come after me, unless the FATHER who sent me draw him,"* Jesus has said. Again, through beautiful parables, and often even without using this means so well known to the people, He teaches us that it is enough to knock and it will be opened, to seek in order to find, and to hold out one's hand humbly to receive what is asked for. He also says that everything we ask the *Father in His name,* He will grant it. No doubt, it is because of this teaching that the Holy Spirit, before Jesus' birth, dictated this prophetic prayer: *"Draw me, we shall run."*

What is it then to ask to be *"Drawn"* if not to be united in an intimate way to the object which captivates our heart? If fire and iron had the use of reason, and if the latter said to the other: "Draw me," would it not prove that it desires to be identified with the fire in such a way that the fire penetrate and drink it up with its burning substance and seem to become one with it? Dear Mother, this is my prayer. I ask Jesus to draw me into the flames of His love, to unite me so closely to Him that He live and act in me. I feel that the more the fire of love burns within my heart, the more I shall say, *"Draw me,"* the more also the souls who will approach me (poor little piece of iron, useless if I withdraw from the divine furnace), the more these souls *will run swiftly in the* [fragrance] *of the ointments of their Beloved,* for a soul that is burning with love cannot remain inactive.

—*Story of a Soul,* 257–58

Act of Oblation to Merciful Love

O My God! Most Blessed Trinity, I desire to *Love* You and make You *Loved*. . . . I feel in my heart immense desires and it is with confidence I ask You to come and take possession of my soul. . . . If through weakness I sometimes fall, may Your *Divine Glance* cleanse my soul immediately, consuming all my imperfections like the fire that transforms everything into itself. . . . In the evening of this life, I shall appear before You with empty hands, for I do not ask You, Lord, to count my works. All our justice is stained in Your eyes. I wish, then, to be clothed in Your own *Justice* and to receive from Your *Love* the eternal possession of *Yourself*. . . .

I OFFER MYSELF AS A VICTIM OF HOLOCAUST TO YOUR MERCIFUL LOVE, asking You to consume me incessantly, allowing the waves of *infinite tenderness* shut up within You to overflow into my soul, and that thus I may become a *martyr* of Your *Love*, O my God!

May this martyrdom, after having prepared me to appear before You, finally cause me to die and may my soul take its flight without any delay into the eternal embrace of *Your Merciful Love*.

I want, O my *Beloved*, at each beat of my heart to renew this offering to You an infinite number of times, until the shadows having disappeared I may be able to tell You of my *Love* in an *Eternal Face to Face!*

—*Story of a Soul*, 276–77

I want to spend my heaven in doing good on earth.

—*St. Thérèse of Lisieux: Her Last Conversations*, 102

Consider!

During the last months of her life, Thérèse discovered yet another aspect of "the science of love." Echoing St. Paul's prayer, "It is no longer I who live, but it is Christ who lives in me," Thérèse explained, "I ask Jesus to draw me into the flames of His love, to unite me so closely to Him that He live and act in me" (SS 257).

"Draw me" expressed Thérèse's powerful, prayerful "surge of the heart" (SS 242; CCC 2558)

"Draw me" voiced her total receptivity to God's merciful love: letting the *Divine Glance* cleanse her soul, consuming all her imperfections.

The Scripture reads, "Draw *me: we* will run" (Song of Solomon 1:3, DR; emphasis added). Noticing that the *me* became *we,* Thérèse understood that when one member of Christ's body is drawn into a deeper love, captivated by the fragrance of God's love, then everyone she loves is also drawn with her into God's love, "without constraint, without effort, it is a natural consequence of her [the soul's] attraction for You" (SS 254)

"Draw me" articulated, then, Thérèse's desire that God not only embrace her but with her gather everyone into his love. "*The zeal of a Carmelite embraces the whole world,*" she wrote, and in her vocation as the loving heart of the mystical body, she desired the salvation of all from the beginning of time until time would be no more (SS 253).

She was further delighted and relieved that she did not even need to use the complete prayer but that the "simple statement: 'Draw me' suffices" (SS 254). Thérèse had discovered a way to pray for those who asked for her prayers even when she forgot who asked her and for what. "Draw me" became Thérèse's prayer, bringing together her yearning to be united more deeply with God and her desire to intercede for others.

"Draw me" voiced her longing to come to God "with empty hands," to descend like Zacchaeus, and like the tax collector, to let God be God in her spiritual poverty (SS 277).

"Draw me" expressed her willingness to empty herself in union with Jesus' self-emptying.

"Draw me" was the blossoming of her prayer during her father's suffering—to love God by letting God love her.

"Draw me" declared her vocation to "*be Love*" at the heart of the Church (SS 194)..

"Draw me" was at the heart of her Act of Oblation to Merciful Love, which she recited often at the end of her life. And during the last months, "Draw me" became Thérèse's treasured prayer words as her breathing became less and less possible.

* * * * * *

Two years before her death, Thérèse learned of a pious prayer becoming popular among Carmelite sisters. The prayer asked God to accept the sisters as substitute victims for sinners who, the sisters thought, deserved divine wrath. In this way, the God of vengeful justice would be appeased (see WLW 165ff).

Thérèse knew that the Father of Jesus was not vengeful and needed no appeasement. So she deliberately composed an Act of Oblation, not to God's justice, but to God's merciful love. In that act, she used the same words used in the pious prayer that spoke of God's violence, but she changed the meaning of the words (see EIG 232ff).

Thus, at the heart of her Act of Oblation to Merciful Love, she prayed: "I OFFER MYSELF AS A VICTIM OF HOLOCAUST TO YOUR MERCIFUL LOVE, asking You to consume me incessantly, allowing the waves of *infinite tenderness* shut up within You to overflow into my soul, and that thus I may become a *martyr* of Your *Love*, O my God!" (SS 277).

She prayed to be "A VICTIM OF HOLOCAUST," but not in the sense of being violently victimized. Rather, praying to be a victim to "MERCIFUL LOVE," she longed to be consumed not by God's wrath but in the flood of God's "*infinite tenderness.*" Thérèse wanted to "become a *martyr*," not through a violent death, but by being drowned in the torrent of God's "*Merciful Love.*" Thérèse prayed to be loved to death.

The Act of Oblation to Merciful Love is the anthem of Thérèse's spirituality, and "Draw me" is the summary and essence of that oblation.

Thérèse's little way is a path of living and dying daily in God's love—attaining holy union with God without violent asceticism, without struggling to climb the illusory stairway of perfection, without laboring up ladders of sanctity, and without needing to appease in any way a wrathful God. Thérèse's way is self-surrender and gratitude, confidence and love. Her spirituality does no violence to herself or to others.

✻ ✻ ✻ ✻ ✻ ✻

On the evening of Holy Thursday in April 1896, Thérèse participated in adoration until midnight and then returned to her cell. As Good Friday began, Thérèse started coughing blood. "*It was like a sweet and distant murmur,*" Thérèse later wrote, "*which announced the Bridegroom's arrival*" (SS 211). She was twenty-three years old and knew she was dying. She was at peace. She had not the least suspicion that she was about to begin eighteen months of excruciating physical, emotional, and spiritual suffering (see EIG 302ff; WLW 195ff).

With the onslaught of tuberculosis, Thérèse's body gradually deteriorated in agonizing pain. In the last weeks, her digestive system completely broke down and her vomiting increased. To the embarrassment of many sisters in the community, she could no longer receive the Eucharist. She coughed almost constantly and struggled to breathe. Totally emptied physically, emotionally, and spiritually, she would finally suffocate.

As Thérèse's physical condition worsened and her pain became overwhelming, her previously stabilized powerful feelings arose with a vengeance. At times she became irritated and impatient. She was plagued with thoughts of being abandoned and isolated. Self-doubt and suicidal impulses surfaced. "Yes!" she whispered to a sister. "What a grace it is to have faith! If I had not had any faith, I would have committed suicide without an instant's hesitation" (HLC 196).

Thérèse saw herself as the scrap of imperfect iron, and God's love was the fire. She desired to be drawn into the fire, to be identified with the fire, and to be purified by the fire. She would "drink it up . . . to become one with it" (SS 257). Thérèse would be plunged into the fire as Joan of Arc had been—drawn into "*the fire of the Divine Love.*"

"What is it then," Thérèse acknowledged in faith, "to ask to be '*Drawn*' if not to be united in an intimate way to the object which captivates our heart?" (SS 257) Thérèse desired to be more deeply united with Christ, who had emptied himself and had become obedient to the point of death. As her heart surged, her lips uttered, "Draw me."

Even though she knew on that Good Friday night that she was dying, she remained at peace. Two days later, on Easter Sunday, as her physical torment began to grip her, a spiritual terror overwhelmed her. She was plunged into inner darkness. A thick fog of confusion blanketed her mind, and a black void opened before her. She was overwhelmed by fright and seized by the terror of meaninglessness, nothingness, and spiritual confusion (see SS 212).

As she slowly wasted away physically and lost control emotionally, she began a solitary, stumbling walk through "a dark tunnel with no light and no end." "The darkest storm; the night of nothingness," she called it—a lonely, painful ordeal of eighteen months, filled with spiritual desolation and anguish. She entered "the trial of faith" (SS 190, 213).

As with her father's dying, now again Thérèse's faith was being tested. And "this trial was to last not a few days or a few weeks," she wrote. "It was not to be extinguished until the hour set by God Himself and this hour has not yet come" (SS 211–12). This hour came only with her final breath.

"Everything has disappeared!" she wrote. A wall of suffering surrounded and isolated her, "a wall which reaches right up to the heavens and covers the starry firmament" (SS 213, 214).

"It seems to me that the darkness . . . says mockingly to me: 'You are dreaming about the light, about a fatherland [heaven],'" she wrote. "[Y]ou are dreaming about the *eternal* possession of the Creator'" (SS 213). She refused to write more, fearing her confusion would further embarrass and scandalize her sisters.

Her most precious desire had been to be drawn into the presence of God "in an *Eternal Face to Face*" (SS 277). Now God and heaven had disappeared. Her desire to share God's love eternally appeared illusory; her treasured longing to spend her heaven "doing good on earth," a flimsy dream (CCC 956). Would she ever see her beloved Jesus, his treasured Mother Mary, or even her dear human family?

She began to doubt her own sincerity. Her little way of spirituality vanished. Her faith vision disappeared in the darkness. She wondered if her years had been wasted in self-delusion. Thoughts of suicide recurred. Yet she continued, the best she could, on the path of faith and love, creating that path as she walked it.

In the inscrutable ways of God's mercy, Thérèse was being purified of any trace of vanity, self-centeredness, and egotism.

* * * * * *

During her last distressing months, Thérèse's feelings united her with unbelievers. She referred to atheists as her "brothers." Now, far from expecting to enjoy heaven's eternal banquet, she consented to dine with atheists and agnostics, willing "to eat the bread of sorrow" as long as God willed. She would find her place at "this table filled with bitterness," where "poor sinners are eating," until the day determined by God (SS 212). Eating their bread, Thérèse could pray with unbelievers and sinners as one of them, loving them compassionately on their own terms.

At the same time, she saw herself united with Jesus in his experience of spiritual darkness and isolation, praying with

Jesus in total self-emptying: "My God, my God why have you forsaken me?" She was willingly participating in the paschal mystery, in Jesus' redemptive suffering for the world. She was being Love at the heart of the mystical body, participating in and "completing what is lacking in Christ's afflictions for the sake of his body, that is, the church" (Colossians 1:24).

Devoid of any felt sense of God's presence, with heaven walled from her, with her deepest longing disappearing, Thérèse still clung to love—to surrendering to God's love for her. She continued to write prayers and poetry as the sisters requested, but she admitted, "When I sing of the happiness of heaven and of the eternal possession of God, I feel no joy in this, for I sing simply what I WANT TO BELIEVE" (SS 214).

Thérèse was suffering a "trial of faith" that ironically became the occasion for her to deepen her spirit of faith, multiplying her acts of faith. "Since the time He permitted me to suffer temptations against the *faith*," she wrote, "He has greatly increased the *spirit of faith* in my heart." "I believe I have made more acts of faith in this past year than all through my whole life" (SS 219, 213; EIG 271ff; WLW 195ff).

"Draw me" led her into a new depth of loving faith by the very trial of faith.

In her last agony, Thérèse whispered, "I am not sorry for delivering myself up to Love. Oh! no, I'm not sorry; on the contrary!" Her final sigh echoed her entire life: "Oh, I love Him! My God, . . . I love You!" (HLC 205–6)

Thérèse's early desire to love God by surrendering herself and being drawn into God's mercy, as the tax collector and Zacchaeus had, was fulfilled. Thérèse's love had become the simple willingness to welcome God's love in the unfolding of divine providence, in the present moment of her dying. Her response was "Draw me."

Thérèse died September 30, 1897, about 7:20 in the evening. God had drawn her into the flames of his love. She had become a "martyr of [Divine] Love" (SS 277). As she so desired, God loved her to death.

Understand!

1. Thérèse's trial of faith echoed Jesus' prayer on the cross: "My God, my God, why have you forsaken me?" (Matthew 27:46). Have you made acts of faith during times of spiritual aridity or suffering, when you had no sense of God's love for you? What was that like? How did your faith response in spite of your circumstances affect you?

_____

_____

_____

_____

_____

2. Thérèse relates her prayer, "Draw me," to certain Scripture passages. How do you think those passages helped her to understand her prayer as "simple" and sure to draw God's love (see John 6:44; Matthew 7:7; John 15:16)? How do

Scripture and Thérèse's prayer inspire you to pray in simple confidence for others?

_____

_____

_____

_____

_____

3. What do you believe was behind Thérèse's courage to compose her bold Act of Oblation to Merciful Love when popular piety spoke of appeasing God's wrath? What passages of Scripture help you appreciate her confidence in God's "waves of *infinite tenderness*" (SS 277)?

_____

_____

_____

_____

_____

4. How would you express Thérèse's certainty that the "*Divine Glance*" cleansed her soul "immediately, consuming all my imperfections like the fire that transforms everything into itself" (SS 276)? Have you noticed passages in Scripture that confirm Thérèse's confidence?

_____

_____

_____

_____

_____

Reflect!

1. What do you think were some of Thérèse's expectations as she was dying? In what ways do you see her responding to her changing circumstances? How have you seen the mysterious, creative ways of God bypassing Thérèse's expectations but fulfilling her real hopes?

_____

_____

_____

_____

_____

2. Thérèse, in composing her Act of Oblation, changed the meaning of some pious words that ordinarily have violent overtones: *martyr, oblation, holocaust, consume.* In what ways did she also change the meaning of *perfection, mortification, sacrifice,* and *dying daily?*

_____

_____

_____

_____

_____

3. Considering that Thérèse is such a great saint, how do you respond to her having ideas of suicide? In what ways do you see these ideas and other aspects of her trial of faith affecting her compassion for those without faith?

_____

_____

_____

_____

_____

4. How would you explain the fact that when Thérèse composed pious prayers and poetry during her trial of faith, she was not being deceptive? Keeping her approach in mind, how do you strike a balance between maintaining an uncomplaining attitude in trials and being honest about those trials?

_____

_____

_____

_____

_____

Act!

Thérèse understood that "dying daily" was not about inflicting painful, punitive penances on herself but about practicing the necessary self-disciplines to do small, inconspicuous acts of charity, of forgiving and asking forgiveness. Going forward, how will you let Thérèse's little way influence your spiritual practice?

Summary and Conclusion

By naming Thérèse a doctor of the Church, Pope St. John Paul II clearly signaled that Thérèse's spirituality is the official teaching of the Church, not marginal, passing, or reserved for a special group. Her life and wisdom form a timely, understandable proclamation of the Gospel for all the faithful and for the world.

Thérèse's faith vision, as we have seen in these sessions, emphasizes aspects of the Gospel and holiness that were lost under the impact of heresies and mistaken ideas about God's love that lingered from earlier times. Among important aspects of her message that were noted in these sessions:

- Thérèse understood that Gospel holiness, revealed by Jesus, did not require moral perfection but rather promoted authentic love.
- Thérèse's life revealed that spiritual growth was not according to schedule but gradual and disappointingly painful, requiring her to love herself with the same patience, kindness, and perseverance that Jesus practiced toward sinners.
- Thérèse continually prayed, questioned, and searched the Church's teaching, the Scriptures, Tradition, and her own experiences to discern "the science of love."
- Thérèse taught, as Jesus revealed, that the heavenly Father is a "God for us," a God on our side, a God with us, a God of unconditional, persevering love, without revenge or violence—a God who empowers us to love as God loves.
- Thérèse modeled how to live Jesus' unique new commandment by loving her "enemies" with forbearance and forgiveness and without retaliation.

- Thérèse noticed and taught that self-awareness freed her from some blind spots and empowered her to love more authentically. She recognized that blind spots often resulted from being overpowered by her compulsive thoughts and excessive feelings. At such times, she tended to act without inner freedom, and lacking this freedom, she stumbled onto the path of violence. She regained her footing on the path of love through vigilance, prayer, patience, prudence, perseverance, and practices of charity.

- Thérèse recognized from her experience six psychological heart qualities that prompted her on the path of love: (1) inner freedom; (2) compassion; (3) creativity; (4) a spirit of willingness; (5) self-surrender; and (6) gratitude.

- Thérèse practiced two steps in walking her little way of love, steps that she took over and over: (1) becoming aware of her weakness and mixed motivation; and (2) being willing to repent and surrender into God's providence.

- Thérèse was bold and assertive, but she recognized that if she acted willfully, bullying herself or others, even with good intentions and for spiritual purposes, she acted in violence and from disguised ego. This alerted her to bypass her ego drive by doing inconspicuous and small acts of charity—little things with great love.

- Thérèse's awareness and boldness prompted her to change the meaning of some spiritual terms, such as *perfection, sacrifice, mortification, self-discipline, ascetical practices, offering it up, spiritual martyrdom, being consumed, offering oneself as a victim of holocaust*, and *dying daily*. In the ordinary spiritual teaching of her times, these and other such terms implied violence to oneself or to others, often to appease God's wrath.

Thérèse's teaching changed all such terms to eliminate any semblance of violence and to mean loving cooperation with God's love.

- Thérèse came to understand and participate as fully as she could in the one great circle of God's love flowing through the mystical body.

These were some of Thérèse's teachings and practices that reveal a Gospel love understandable and attainable in our time. In this way, she spoke to today's spiritual questions: "How does one live a human life fully and well?" and "What does being a holy person look like today?" Thérèse's life and faith vision addressed these questions on the personal level, from the microcosm of her cloistered life, and implicitly on the social and cultural level as well.

On her deathbed, Thérèse said that she would spend her heaven "doing good on earth" (SS 102). That good is not only the many minor and major coincidences and salvific responses her devotees continue to experience. It is also her gift of revealing a faith vision of meaning, goodness, joy, and peace, as well as identifying heart qualities and providing practices supporting a path of love that is accessible and healing in our times of spiritual confusion and violence.

The final reflection and question is then: "What aspects of Thérèse's life of faith affirm you, and what aspects challenge you?" Or specifically, "What are you called to do now?"

_____
_____
_____
_____

Select Bibliography

Bro, Bernard. *Saint Thérèse of Lisieux: Her Family, Her God, Her Message*. San Francisco: Ignatius Press, 2003.

de Meester, Conrad, OCD. *With Empty Hands: The Message of Saint Thérèse of Lisieux*. Washington, DC: ICS Publications, 2002.

Descouvemont, Pierre. *Thérèse of Lisieux and Marie of the Trinity: The Transformative Relations of Saint Thérèse of Lisieux and Her Novice Sister Marie of the Trinity*. New York: Alba House, 1997.

John Paul II, *Divini Amoris Scientia*, Apostolic Letter Proclaiming St. Thérèse of the Child Jesus and the Holy Face a Doctor of the Universal Church, October 19, 1997.

O'Mahony, Christopher, OCD, ed. and trans. *St. Thérèse of Lisieux by Those Who Knew Her*. Huntington, IN: Our Sunday Visitor, 1975.

Schmidt, Joseph F., FSC. *Everything Is Grace: The Life and Way of Thérèse of Lisieux*. Frederick, MD: The Word Among Us Press, 2007.

———. *Praying with Thérèse of Lisieux*. Frederick, MD: The Word Among Us Press, 1991.

———. *Walking the Little Way of Thérèse of Lisieux: Discovering the Path of Love*. Frederick, MD: The Word Among Us Press, 2012.

Thérèse of Lisieux. *Collected Poems of St. Thérèse of Lisieux*. Translated by Alan Bancroft. Herefordshire, England: Gracewing, 2001.

———. *General Correspondence, Volumes I and II*. Translated by John Clarke, OCD. Washington, DC: ICS Publications, 1982, 1988.

———. *St. Thérèse of Lisieux: Her Last Conversations*. Translated by John Clarke, OCD. Washington, DC: ICS Publications, 1977.

———. *Story of a Soul*. Translated by John Clarke, OCD. Washington, DC: ICS Publications, 1977.

Acknowledgments

Quotations from *Story of a Soul*, translated by John Clarke, OCD. Copyright © 1975, 1976, 1996, by Washington Province of Discalced Carmelites, ICS Publications, 2131 Lincoln Road, N.E., Washington, D.C. 20002-1199 U.S.A. www.icspublications.org. Used with permission.

Quotations from *St. Thérèse of Lisieux: Her Last Conversations*, translated by John Clarke, OCD. Copyright © 1977, Washington Province of Discalced Carmelites, ICS Publications, 2131 Lincoln Road, N.E., Washington, D.C. 20002-1199 U.S.A. www.icspublications.org. Used with permission.

Quotations from *General Correspondence, Volume One*, translated by John Clarke, OCD. Copyright © 1982 by Washington Province of Discalced Carmelites, ICS Publications, 2131 Lincoln Road, N.E., Washington, D.C. 20002-1199 U.S.A. www.icspublications.org. Used with permission.

Quotations from *General Correspondence, Volume Two*, translated by John Clarke, OCD. Copyright © 1988 by Washington Province of Discalced Carmelites, ICS Publications, 2131 Lincoln Road, N.E., Washington, D.C. 20002-1199 U.S.A. www.icspublications.org. Used with permission.

Quotations from *Thérèse of Lisieux and Marie of the Trinity*, by Pierre Descouvemont, translated by Alexandra Plettenberg-Serban. Copyright © 1997 by the Society of St. Paul.

The *Spirit* of Catholic Living

T his book was published by The Word Among Us. Since 1981, The Word Among Us has been answering the call of the Second Vatican Council to help Catholic laypeople encounter Christ in the Scriptures.

The name of our company comes from the prologue to the Gospel of John and reflects the vision and purpose of all of our publications: to be an instrument of the Spirit, whose desire is to manifest Jesus' presence in and to the children of God. In this way, we hope to contribute to the Church's ongoing mission of proclaiming the gospel to the world so that all people would know the love and mercy of our Lord and grow more deeply in their faith as missionary disciples.

Our monthly devotional magazine, *The Word Among Us*, features meditations on the daily and Sunday Mass readings, and currently reaches more than one million Catholics in North America and another half million Catholics in one hundred countries around the world. Our book division, The Word Among Us Press, publishes numerous books, Bible studies, and pamphlets that help Catholics grow in their faith.

To learn more about who we are and what we publish, log on to our website at www.wau.org. There you will find a variety of Catholic resources that will help you grow in your faith.

Embrace His Word, Listen to God . . .

www.wau.org